Nothing But God

A True Story

by
Anthony Calloway

Bloomington, IN Milton Keynes, UK

AuthorHouse™
1663 Liberty Drive, Suite 200
Bloomington, IN 47403
www.authorhouse.com
Phone: 1-800-839-8640

AuthorHouse™ UK Ltd.
500 Avebury Boulevard
Central Milton Keynes, MK9 2BE
www.authorhouse.co.uk
Phone: 08001974150

For speaking engagements
contact: Anthony Calloway
email: warrecon2@verizon.net

© 2007 Anthony Calloway. All rights reserved.

No part of this book may be reproduced, stored in a retrieval system, or transmitted by any means without the written permission of the author.

First published by AuthorHouse 4/30/2007

ISBN: 978-1-4259-8960-6 (sc)

Library of Congress Control Number: 2007900513

Printed in the United States of America
Bloomington, Indiana

This book is printed on acid-free paper.

Dedication

When I was in the "world" I had always heard talk of angels but I never thought I would have one to call my own. But God blessed me with a true angel and I am so proud to have her as my wife. Karen, is a woman of deep faith who stood strong on her biblical values. She never left me or abandoned me through all of my faults, trials and tribulations. Through my sickness and disease my wife was strong. She had faith and courage that no one else could see. Karen was there for her children providing for them and often neglecting her own needs. She is a praying and faithful woman of God. Even when I lost my mind from liver disease, cursed her daily and told her "just let me die" she was still there. Things got so bad I told the medical staff that she was no longer in charge of me and that I was capable of making sound medical decisions on my own. After telling her that I hated her, she was still there. I honor you, Karen. I pray to only true and living God that he may provide a special place for you in heaven. Job well done my wife may God keep and bless you for the days to come.

My dear children I thank God for you guys. You were there to change my diapers, you hand fed me, prayed with and for me, helped mommy wash my body, and you were there to console me in the midnight hours. I know you can remember spending long days and nights in emergency rooms. May God have favor on your lives. All the hell you had to endure and you are still in your right "state of mind". I also cursed you children daily; Daddy was not only sick in the body but the mind and soul as well. I love you guys, and I dedicate this book to my children also. I am proud to call myself your Father.

Foreword

Anthony Calloway's first book "Nothing but God" a true story is a testimony to the Lord's mercy and grace.

Born and raised in a middle class family in Newark, New Jersey, Anthony was taught the ethics of hard work and solid family values. After serving in the Marine Corps and returning home his life began to veer out of control, thereby like so many, becoming a father far too early and the drama continued.

In his very poignant testimonial he speaks of the pitfall of pride, arrogance and being ignorant on purpose! Yet by the grace and mercy of God he stands today as a faithful husband and father and a testimony to true manhood on his job, community and his church.

As his pastor I have watched him endure great pain and sickness with terminal liver disease, which was reversed miraculously by a liver transplant that was provided at the eleventh hour. Anthony recognizes that he has been given another chance so that he might not only raise his family, but raise up a generation to finish the race. We are facing a generation of children who are insolent, bruised, broken, and in many cases rebellious. Sadly, the family and family life has broken down to such a degree that far too many of our children have been left as casualties.

I want to commend Anthony on his first book and encourage all who read it to think about the Lord's goodness and grace. It is the Lord's grace and mercy that keeps us all standing, moving and pressing our way.

Indeed, "in Him we live and move and have our being." Congratulations to Anthony Calloway in this beginning of a wonderful journey. I commend him to the world.

Bishop Donald Hilliard, Jr.
Sr. Pastor Cathedral International

Acknowledgement Page

To: Monique Moore I truly thank you for putting your pen where my mouth was and becoming the wind beneath my wings. You have helped me soar beyond my imagination. Thank you for dreaming for me and believing that this story needed to be heard. It was nothing but God that "inspired you to inspire" me to begin this book.

To: Margaret Johnson Mills Thank you my sister for allowing God to use you in my most critical time of need. Your unselfishness to my family and I will always be remembered. I pray that God continues to use you to bring people closer to him.

To: Medina Hopper I just want to thank you my cousin for your true devotion and hard work with your editorial skills in the development of my manuscript. May God's grace and mercy continue to shine upon you, and draw you closer to him.

To: Bishop Donald Hilliard Jr. My Spiritual father, my Shepherd. I thank God for you Bishop. You are a man with integrity, a visionary, and a profit. Bishop, your preaching and teaching has helped me become a better man, a better husband to my wife, a better father to my children, and a better son. You have inspired me in so many ways. The Bible says Faith comes by hearing and hearing the word of the Lord.

Introduction

Has your mortality ever been tested? Have you ever had a close call? Have you ever been so physically sick or seriously injured that you didn't think that you would recover? Do you know what it is like to have a second chance at life?

Here it is July 8, 2002, my wife and I are preparing to take what I thought would be my final vacation. My liver was no longer functioning and the disease had ravaged my body. I had lost hope and I had no faith. I was told by my doctors that I would not survive another month without a liver transplant. What shall I do? All I wanted to do in my last days was to make sure that I spent some quality time with my wife and kids. At 6 a.m. that morning I received a phone call from Thomas Jefferson University Hospital in Philadelphia, PA advising me that they had found a perfect match for my liver transplant. They described the organ as a Lexus vehicle; they compared the condition of the organs to vehicles. But the enemy of my soul told me that I did not need the life saving transplant. I decided to live out my last days however God would see fit. He didn't care about me anyway, why would I be facing this if God really cared? The transplant surgeon informed me that I had three hours to get to the hospital to undergo my life saving liver transplant. But before I hung up the phone I told the surgeon I was on my way to a funeral. He advised me that if I didn't make it there in 3 hours or less it was going to be my funeral that my family members would be attending. At that point I hung up the phone and proceeded to take my wife on vacation at whatever cost.........

Chapter 1

IN THE BEGINNING

I was born July 27, 1959 in the city of Newark, NJ. My parents were hard working old school parents. I was the youngest out of 2 children between the union of my father, Herbert R. Calloway, Sr. and my mother Helen Calloway. My mother had a child from her first marriage by the name of Jacqueline, we called her Jackie. She was 10 years my senior and she was a loving sister. Herbert R. Calloway, Jr. known today as Jamaal, is the middle child. We were a close family, never really needing anything. We were a typical middle class family living in the city of Newark in the early sixties. My dad worked for General Motors and later on became a Newark Special Police Officer.

My mother worked as a dairy worker for Farmstead Dairy. After graduating from Weequahic High School and having no one to inspire me to further my education, I joined the United States Marine Corps along with several of my childhood friends. My first duty station was Marine Corps Recruit Depot (MCRD) San Diego, Calif. Boot camp was 16 weeks of grueling hell! and I must truly say to you that even though my father prepared me for manhood, I really feel that my drill instructors in the USMC made a man out of me. They took me to the next level in a way that no parent ever could. After traveling half way around the world, up and down Southeast Asia receiving medals and commendations, I was void in the spirit.

The year is now 1982 and I had just been discharged from the USMC. I was a young man in need of civil direction. I had no job and I was back home living with my parents. My first civilian job began in 1983 at the Newark Stamp and Stationary. I earned $3.50 an hour $114.00 a week and still paid my parents rent and provided for myself. Six months after my employment with the stamp and stationary store the Lord blessed me with a security job which paid an additional 90 cents an hour. I was still void in the spirit and not thanking God for the blessing that he bestowed on me. But even with all of my faults God continued to bless me.

Now I am working 2 jobs one during the day and one during the midnight hours. Shortly after that I was blessed again with a job working with New Jersey Transit Railroad Division cleaning toilets at Newark's Penn Station at the rate of $7.00 an hour. Still not praising God from where he brought me and keeping a roof over my head. No I was not making top dollar, but it was better than what I had been making. I did not mind cleaning toilets and scrubbing floors, it was an honest day's work. Something that people today, especially younger people should consider.

The year now is 1984 and I have become somewhat promiscuous. I started dating and not making commitments I became involved in a relationship with one young lady whom I impregnated. Through that union my daughter was born. She was born on March 13, 1984, my first child whom I love until this day. Her mother and I did not get far in our relationship. I was 25 years old and I did not know what a relationship was all about and besides that I was too hot to settle down. I wanted to continue to date women without being tied down to one. I supported my daughter, loved her, took care of her while her mother worked and went to school. I never neglected my responsibilities as a father but yet still not being faithful to the woman who had my child.

After years and years of baby mama drama, my daughter's mother and I began a hateful relationship; the devil had just taken over. Here I am still void in the spirit, she was also void, thus allowing Satan to step in and do what he does best. Our relationship grew bitter and became so bad that whenever a woman came in contact with me, and she would find out, it would be on! She would torment me and these women because of her bitterness and pain. She would deny my visitation rights all because of this young black man by the name of Anthony Calloway who stepped into her life, impregnated her and left her high and dry. Oh God, not knowing what I know now, I do repent and that is the problem today; young boys are going out impregnating these young girls. This vicious cycle must stop, we must teach our children to be responsible if you lay you stay! Marry that man or woman first before you think about making a family. Oh yes I can say it because I am reaping what I sowed, my daughter born March 13, 1984 is now a mother at the age of 20, facing baby mama drama and where is my baby's daddy? What goes around comes around. In this text you will learn from me and the mistakes that I have made. But in despite of all of my faults, I am still one of God's anointed and because of that and what you are about to read further on, it still worked out for my good because I love the Lord so much now he leads me to greener pastures.

Chapter 2

LIFE IN THE FAST LANE

The year now is 1985, May 1985 to be exact. I just got hired at The United States Post Office. After waiting on the list for 2 years and having Veteran Status I finally got the job at the Main Post office as a Mail handler. I was making close to $9.00 an hour. God has really been good to me, even with all of my issues and my praise less behind. The Lord still did not forsake me, but when will I cry out to the Lord? No time soon because everything in my life is running so smooth. I felt that there was no reason to praise him. I was assigned to the midnight shift that still allowed me to keep my job at NJ Transit and work midnights at the Post Office. I was going around calling myself "Anwar Sadat" a man of peace thinking that I was a Muslim but never attending a prayer meeting or Masjid. I was just going along with the fad. You see this is what we did in Newark back then, changing our names, obtaining attributes and as a child I was pressured to follow my family as they went in and out of bags. First we were Baptist, then we were Catholics, then we wore Dashiki's and African beads and it was all about black power and the black movement. Half of my family switched to the Nation of Islam and stopped eating pork, and I was told that the white man was the devil. I was so confused, grown folks be very careful about what you say and do around young people, they like to emulate what they see and they listen very closely. My family sent me mixed messages.

Now getting back to the Post Office, which in 1985 had a whole lot of fringe benefits and I'm not talking about 401k plans and paid vacations. I'm talking about women, sex, drugs, alcohol, gambling and backbiting, just a real cesspool…still void and confused in the spirit. I was going around saying I was a Muslim never praying to Allah or God, I became entrapped into the devil's party and I was the honoree, going straight to hell, caught up with all the intangibles. But now I know in the year 2006, and you can't say that you know unless you've witnessed or been in the fire and you see the right hand of God pull you through. Now Satan the enemy of my soul has started to consume every aspect of my life in some sort of way. I was content with my worldly ways, constantly being consumed with a materialistic lifestyle, while continuously being set up by the devil. I find myself getting more involved in the devil's play. I started hanging out with the wrong crowd, but still being watched over by the Lord's angels, every time as I stepped into go-go bars or having unprotected sex. I was running the streets like a wolf stalking prey, being involved in such activities that I am ashamed to write about. But with all of my issues the Lord saves his anointed. I was always a good person at heart, always taking care of my mother and being obedient to my parents and elders. I was not a troublemaker. I was a humble likeable young man, a hardworking man, a class act, but I was constantly living in sin.

I was offered an acting supervisor's job with the Post Office, again being set up by the devil. Now I find myself sitting around the round table with upper management whom most of them were the devil in disguise. I started to carry out some of their plans. They changed my perception of the whole business. They built a sense of character in me to be like Teflon. At this particular time they were looking for "Cold Leaders", leaders that would not care about the people, it was all about the numbers, but I couldn't see it then. I took this thing serious, I just wanted to be in and I would do anything to stay in grace with the powers to be. I was a good candidate, a fresh young military man someone whom they knew would carry out all of their orders and take no prisoners. Someone who only cared about themselves, and did not care who they had to step on to get where they wanted to go and that is to the top. Corporate America portrays to the people that is the place to be, no matter how you get there and no matter what it takes; selling your soul, selling your body, it doesn't matter! Everyone wants to be on the top. Will being on the top make you happy? Will it bring you closer to the Lord? My answer now is no, because going through what I went through and seeing what I have seen my worship is now for real. You don't know my story but as you read on you will know why I love the Lord so much. I now find myself being liked by the powers that be. They were using me and I was using them. We were bed partners, the Postal Service upper management was screwing me and I was screwing them back (not literally), oh we made a good team together. I began to bring on enemies; co-workers who were seeing me rise to the top. Jealous managers who knew that I had the potential to lead an entire facility, I was caught up in the mix of it all. I began to run every operation in the Post Office. I was getting the numbers; I was writing letters of warnings and giving out suspensions. All this power went straight to my head. I became entrapped into the business. I slept the P.O. and I ate the P.O., this was my life and all along God has other plans for me.

The year now is 1987, my sister's health had began to decline. She was becoming heavily involved in drugs with her husband (who is now deceased). Back on smack or did she ever leave it alone. Year's prior they held down professional jobs and were responsible. After watching my sister get off drugs and then turn herself over to the Lord, this still did not send any flashing lights in my head that it should now be my time. Oh no not me! Too busy holding down my spot at the P.O. Too busy riding around in my brand new Mazda 626, too busy chilling in my bachelors crib, too busy doing all of the other things, I did not have time for God. I remember how my mother would beg me to go to church with her and my sister but the P.O. was more important especially if there was overtime involved. The devil really knows your weakness and mine was power and money. If I had to write my mother up I would to satisfy the service. As my sisters' health begins to decline even further, I begin to grow more apart if it was not about me or what was in it for me I did not want any part of it. After seeing my mother become broken, after my sisters' rapid decline in health the Holy Spirit was trying to move my emotions from being cold and bitter and not caring. After seeing my mother go through breast cancer at the age of 12, and witnessing how God saved her life even though she had to lose both of her breasts due to cancer I was distraught, confused and angry over the fact that this had to happen to my mother. You see back then in 1973 it was very uncommon for breast cancer in the African American community opposed to how it is today in 2006. Seeing my mother become closer to God at that time I could not understand at the age of 12. Helen Calloway called on the Lord and he kept cancer out of her body for the next 31 years of her life. She was cancer free; my mother had begun her new walk with Christ born again. For me, still void in the spirit everything is fine in the life of Anthony Calloway. One afternoon on June 20, 1988 while I was at work at the Post Office, I received a phone call from St. Michael's hospital advising me to report there as soon as possible. When I arrived I was greeted by my mother and my nephew, my sister's only child. They informed me that my sister Jackie was on her way out. I could not grasp the severity because lets face it I have been living in a corporate, materialistic and selfish world. I knew my sister had been in the hospital, but did I ever go by there to pay her a visit or tell her I loved her. Yes sickness and disease had taken over her body, and yes I saw the last breath of life come out her mouth, and yes

I had just witnessed my sister die in front of me. Do you know how that made me feel? Carrying the weight of the world on my shoulders! When will I cry out to the Lord? We buried Jackie on Friday June 24, 1988 as I sat in the front pew with my mother in hand I began to feel something come over me inside that sanctuary. It was the Holy Spirit but I rebuked the spirit. The devil had its grips on me, going on with my career seeing my mother get sick and weak over the loss of my sister but also seeing her go to church two and three times a week and twice on Sunday. I would actually make fun of her. I would say, "Hey ma going back for overtime, wow that preacher has really got you going" and all along Ma is in church praying for Jamaal, dad and I. She would always tell us that she is living a slow death; you see diabetes has now set into her body and it's starting to raise havoc on her. She would ask me to take time off to spend it with her. But my excuse was the P.O., they needed me and the place can't run without me. That place was my God and my family the J-O-B! The Post Office was my God, so I thought. But I am so glad that my mother took the time out to pray me through all my faults. Yes I was a good son and yes I loved my mother when will God open up my eyes. But first, sometimes God has to rearrange your furniture to get you in the right place.

The year now is 1993 and I have now taken a Supervisory detail at the Main P.O. "Opening Unit" in charge of 35 employees and one of these employees would soon become my wife. Still running things in the P.O. so I thought all along God is in control. But you could not tell me that back in 1993. I was one of the star players for the P.O. football team. I was setting traps and checking them, this was my method of getting women. I would bait them and trap them into my web using my position on the job. I used my materialistic possessions such as cars, money and my apartment. Oh I thought I was a player but let me tell you something every player one day will get played. I thought I could trap this one particular young lady who was sent to work with me because her unit had become phased out. I wanted her to become my new victim and eventually trap her into my web like I did so many others. I had actually known this young lady since the 60's; we attended St. Peter's catholic school together. However, she was 3 years my junior and girls were the furthest thing from my mind. She also lived around the corner from me. Back then while the boys played sports and ran the streets she was locked down behind a fence because her parents had plans for her and her sister.

Well back to the Post Office, where I had reacquainted myself with this particular young lady and started to really take a liking to her I found out that she had recently separated from her husband and was awaiting a divorce. Meanwhile, I was engaged to get married in the spring of 1993. Oh boy I am really confused now! I like this new young lady but I love my fiancée and my flesh was becoming weaker for other women. While in my relationship with my fiancée there were so many nice girls who had crossed my path and I must say that I cheated and had sex with a few of them. The devil really had my number, he lived through me. I was cruel at times, disrespectful, nasty, and totally selfish towards women and I mean to tell you there were some nice young ladies. Then there were times when I was a loveable young man who was clean and decent. Lord Jesus I do repent now of my sins towards these women.

Run DMC was hot, break dancing was the new thing and playing as many women as you can get was in. I'm talking about the mid 80's and early 90's and this is what was going on in my hood. Now in this day and time the devil is destroying our youth with gangster rap, violence, gangs, drugs, drive-by's, down-low life styles. I'm calling for all you readers to please help make a difference in some of these young folk's lives. What is so amazing is that God is still watching over me as I travel down this dark road.

Chapter 3

A Divine Relationship

Now this young lady and I have now become somewhat of a hot commodity at the P.O. All of my ex's are trying to destroy our relationship. There was a lot of backbiting going on. Words are starting to be exchanged; folks are whispering in her ear about my past, folks are whispering in my ear about her past. But as I see it today God was in the midst of it all preparing the perfect relationship for me. Yes I had some past issues with women and yes I was a "playa" and yes the nay sayers were busy saying negative things. God knew that this was the start of the process. This young lady and I began to dream about our future. I shared some of my dreams with her and she began sharing her dreams with me. I wanted a wife that would not run the streets like the other women did, and I wanted a wife who would be willing to travel the world with me and share some of my values. But what about my fiancée? Our relationship was played out after the good times were over. This new young lady was taught well and knew how to set up house. She would help me clean, cook good dinners, and would also help me wash my clothes. She was everything I wanted in a woman. She had a few issues that after a while came to pass as well as my issues. I wanted to be a one woman's man so I broke the news to my fiancée that it was over between us. I knew I had hurt her so much, I am truly sorry for the pain I caused her. She taught me so much. She taught me how to grow, how to establish credit and how to pay my bills on time. But God had not given this relationship destiny; she will always have a special place in my heart, her and her family. Karen and I are now starting to go steady. Her marriage is now over and my engagement is now a thing of the past. Karen now is left with a one-year-old son and I am left with a dismantled bachelor pad. The playa lifestyle had come to an end, Thanks be to God. Honestly, I was tired of that lifestyle. Karen told me to give up the bachelor's pad and move in with her and her son. Karen's plan was for us to save money and move out of the city. So I agreed, you know I wanted to see what the "playing house" thing was all about. In the back of my mind I said, "if this did not work out

I could resume my old lifestyle." But God had a plan and purpose for me; I began to enjoy the family setting, something I missed with my fiancée. Jihad, Karen's son was cool and my daughter had taken a liking to him, so we were one big happy family. But Karen was not satisfied she wanted a commitment, but I protested, "no baby everything is fine just the way it is", so she brushed it off for a while. Then I believe the Holy Spirit started to step in. Now knowing what I know it was nothing but God who delivered me from being a player. It was nothing but God who reacquainted Karen and I after 24 years of not seeing each other. The last time I saw Karen she was in the first grade at St. Peter's with snot running down her nose and I was a handsome young fellow in the fourth grade. But, can't you see how God has been faithful to me and at this particular time I will not give him the praise, still void in the spirit. So now God is starting to work on me a bit I am in an exclusive relationship with Karen, I am growing more as an adult and my desires are different. Karen and I began to search for a house. After months of searching we found a home. I was really in love with this girl so why not take this to the next level?

Karen and I got married on June 10, 1995 in my parent's backyard. I remember the day as if it were yesterday. It was a cloudy Saturday; I designed the wedding, a semi-military, African affair. I never realized that God was delivering me then, I had no bachelor's party, I had not cheated on Karen since the day I met her, and I was proud of myself. But you know the devil always wants to steal your joy. My daughter's mother refused to let her participate in the wedding so I was actually hurt on my special day because my baby girl was not there. Hurt and broken the wedding went on as scheduled. June 10, 1995 when Karen and I were married and took our vows for better or worse she was serious. As you read on you will see that Karen stood strong on her biblical vows. God had given me a special gift in Karen that I could not see then. She was like a Christmas gift that you did not open on Christmas day. After 7 years I realized that our marriage, not the wedding was the miracle. Anyone can have a wedding but only God can create a marriage. But I was still not in a hurry to open up my gift that God had sent. I was still busy with my career and trying to quickly move up the ladder, or should I say the ladder to hell in a rush. June 1995, married, homeowner, and still void in the spirit. Unknowingly I was still being controlled by the devil, but this time it is not the women, it is not the partying, it is the JOB!

Chapter 4

THE ENEMY ATTACKS

I am now reassigned to a new facility, under a ruthless manager whom I admired at this point in my life. This man ruled with an iron fist, he did not respect or honor God so he was alright with me. Together we made a tandem. He showered me with gifts. His and her watches, money, power, all I had to do was carry out his plans, crush the people make them work harder. He wanted the numbers and he knew I could deliver. He promised me all sorts of advancements in the P.O. never keeping his word, but after all we know that the devil is a liar. He strung me along and I was constantly being set up by the devil. Oh I had the keys to every door, codes to every computer; I had carte blanche so I thought. But because this manager loved women so much I was being used until a woman who was fine enough and was willing to give her body and soul would take over my position. My manager was weak to the flesh and he forgot about the numbers when it came to a piece of behind! But in the meantime it was Anwar Calloway "nobody does it better" that was my motto. Management knew how to pump my head. The employees grew bitter towards me, but I didn't care. I would write them up left and right. I would also curse them out, oh yes I had a history of calling women the "B" word and I wasn't afraid to tell them "go get your husband, get your man". I also ruled with an iron fist. My manager loved it and the employees would write petitions against me. I was like Teflon, it would not stick, and the charges would roll off me. I had a John Gotti type of spirit, I was untouchable. In the meantime my mother's health was declining so now I find myself torn between the job and my mother's declining health. This was any easy decision I will do both I would go and see about my mother because I had the flexibility to do so. Diabetes has just caused my mother to lose a toe. Ma needs me and I am the baby child, the one who she knew she could count on and yes I was there. But was I there enough, at this particular time, no! Ma had constantly asked me to take some time off to spend with her but my answer was "no" the job needs me. I would say to her, "who is going to run the building when I am not there." After all

I thought no one does it better than me. Thank God for the old timers like CC, Amin and Koti. They tried to keep me grounded, sometimes I would listen and sometimes I wouldn't. Brother Amin would always say to me, "Brother don't you keep this job close to your heart." CC would tell me to relax, and I would reply that there is no time to relax. Koti would just laugh at me and tell me that I was a fool. But he also told me that the service did need me because I was a good boss. The employees were just lazy and were never challenged in the past. Koti spoke of my strong attributes, and being from Ghana he saw something in me that no one else could see, not even myself. He said I had the spirit of a lion; he referred to me as "a diamond in the rough". God knew this also; after all he is my creator. But what is my destiny, postmaster or what? I seldom asked myself. Seventy percent of the employees hated me the other thirty percent thought I was the bomb.

The year now is 1998, July 13, 1998 to be exact and my wife Karen has just given birth to our daughter Niya Jayla. Oh what a blessing from God that my mother is still alive to see our new addition to the Calloway clan. My mother was so happy that it added years to her life. The year now is 2000, I am the manager of the year. Oh I was so happy; but my enemies were appearing all over the place. My car was being attacked; my character was trying to be assassinated. I was under full attack. I would find myself coming home stressed out over the job. Grinding my teeth as I slept at night, tossing and turning in my sleep I was in the hell's fire constantly being consumed by Satan.

My mother is in her final stage of diabetes and it is time for her to lose another toe or two. Shortly after the surgery my mother slips into a coma for 10 days. I am still pressing my way to the Post Office 7 years of perfect attendance over 650 hours of sick leave on the books and still will not take a day off for my mother. When will I change and what will it take to make me change. After the 10th day the Lord had released my mother out of that coma. Oh God had beaten me down in those 10 days. All kind of things had gone through my mind.

If I could only talk to my mother one more time. If I could tell my mother that I loved her. I prayed that week and I was so depressed seeing my mother lie in that condition. For days my conscience tore me apart. But God stepped in one more time. Helen had arisen from her coma; now at this time you would think I would have joined a church, right? Wrong, the next day my mother came out of that coma I was off on a cruise, to only return to find out that my mother was placed in a rehab center in Springfield, NJ. She had to get therapy for her foot after her toes had been removed. God started to move me in closer to my mothers needs. Now I was there 24-7 caring for my mother needs. God was now using me to assist my mother. My mother did not have any siblings it was just us and a few of her cousins. My dad was inexperienced with providing Healthcare to her. My brother and I along with our wives were there. I also must mention Berlinda, the mother of my brother's youngest child. She was like a daughter to my mother, she was there even after the split from my brother, and she really hung in there for my mom! May God bless you Berlinda! I remember the times when Jamaal and his wife would pray for my mother beside her bed in the hospital, I would never join in. I told them at one point that this prayer was useless. I wanted them to put their hands to the plow. It seemed that I was always there 24/7. I was witnessing God's work and I did not even know it. But I was still blind and void. My brother and I argued daily over the fact that Jesus is Lord of all Lords and King of all Kings and every knee shall bow and every tongue shall confess this but I was not hearing that. My only concern was who was going to be on the next watch taking care of mommy. I did not know at this time that God was taking care of her all along. My brother had just become saved and he was a fanatic, both him and his wife. Jesus this and Jesus that, and I did not want to hear it anymore. But the prayers of the righteous were answered and ma was soon discharged from the rehabilitative center and started to continue to live her life. Ma was back in Greater Abyssinian Church in the third row praising God. I had resumed doing what I did best, being the boss at the P.O. creating more enemies. The devil is after my life and he wants to destroy me. The devil is out to destroy you too! Now I am finding myself in constant conflict with the employees, back biters, Judas, evil wicked people, crabs in the barrel. Most of them hated the ground that I walked on. I was in the mix with them all going toe to toe and in the meantime the devil is killing and destroying my love ones all around me.

First it was my sister, then it was a close friend of mine whom I miss to this day. Arnold and I both worked for the P.O. we were also neighbors and he was a good person. He was also a good family man, a man who loved his children, but he didn't believe in God. The both of us would make fun of our wives as they pressed their way to the Second Baptist Church in Perth Amboy. Satan had really done Arnold in, killing him inside the family home and I was mad when this happened. I cried so hard for him and I also cried for his wife and their two young daughters. Arnold came to my house 48 hours prior to him taking his own life. I knew Arnold wanted to discuss some issues with me but I refused to answer the door bell. I just did not want to be bothered that day. He was such a good friend of ours. Who would be the next victim that the enemy will kill? Still seeing Karen and Rhonda (Arnolds wife) attend church regularly I still remained void in the spirit. Even after witnessing the devil take Arnold's life, when would I submit to the Lord? Well, evidently no time soon and not as long as the P.O. keeps dangling a carrot in front of me. Satan was continuously setting me up with power, worldly cares. It was not the time for me to submit.

I see now that Karen has become a member of the church. She continues to press her way despite my ridicule. She now has joined partners with another one of her girlfriends. As they attend church regularly they run into my ex-fiancée at church. She and Karen become acquaintances, it seems as though everyone around me is either dying or turning their life over to Christ. When will it be my time? My mother had become ill once again. Mom was so sick and I was now there 24/7. At this time I did not care about the job, it was all about my mother. I remember going to the hospital three and four times a day. I was losing sleep, I had begun to lose my appetite and still to this day I can remember the telephone call from Union Hospital telling me to return back there at once. Ma was now in ICU on a ventilator, the doctors were telling me that this might very well be the end. You know this was not the first time that I heard that before, what they didn't know was that Helen knew Jesus. Only God would determine when her end would arrive. Once again, the prayers of the righteous were heard and answered. Ma was taken off of the ventilator.

Now it is early February 2001 and I had finally taken time off from work to spend with my mother. We had just enjoyed watching the Super Bowl together a week before, just enjoying one another. Karen and I would take her back and forth to the dollar stores and what a sense of humor she had, saved and blessed by God, little did we know that Helen's days were numbered. She was back in the hospital, her leg was amputated and now we were told that congestive heart failure had set in. After spending Saturday at the hospital I went home anticipating seeing her the next day after work. Sunday, March 10, 2001 after working my shift I called my uncle to see if he was ready to go with me to the hospital because I had no time to waste. I wanted to see my mother the plan was to apply shea butter to my mother's now dry skin. He was not quite ready so I went directly to the hospital. The time is now 4:00 p.m. Sunday afternoon, as I walked into the hospital I heard the "code blue" warning and saw all of the hospital staff racing inside my mother's room. As I enter the room I realize that they were working on my mother and one of the nurses quickly rushes me out into the hallway. My first reaction was not very panicky as I witnessed this before. I looked to my right and saw my mother's cousin sitting in the hallway crying, she was in the room just before my arrival and the two of them were talking. Exhausted they both dozed off; when she awakened she realized that my mother was not responsive. My mother had already passed away, the staff tried to bring her back but she had already gone home to Jesus. I reentered the room and saw my mother lying there so peaceful; she just like my sister had died in front of my eyes. Oh Lord what will I do now? I proceeded to call my dad and my brother, just then Karen walked through the door. I told her "ma is gone".

We buried my mother on March 16, 2001. To God be the glory, no more pain, no more suffering. During the eulogy the minister ended by saying, "Job well done, Helen". I know my mother the late Helen Calloway who went home to be with the Lord at the age of seventy-six is in heaven looking down on all of us. Still void in the spirit and grieving hard I began to lose weight, and I mean rapidly. I weighed 165 lbs before my mother's death. Thirty days later I weigh 145 lbs, but I just blamed it on my grief. I now was the one who needed medical help; I had not been sick in over twenty years and even then only for minor illnesses. Karen and I needed to first find a doctor. The doctor recommended several blood tests that determined that my liver enzymes were slightly elevated. The doctor stated that perhaps it was related to stress and to return the next week for further test, HIV and Hepatitis. I was exhausting my sick time at work. This was the first time in seven years that I used a sick day.

Chapter 5

The Nightmare

Now I am feeling weak, nauseous, and my vision is distorted. I report back to the doctor and he tells me that my liver enzymes are still elevated and he must refer me to a gastroenterologist. At this point I could not grasp the severity of my illness and before I could get in to see the specialist my stomach began to swell like a woman who was 6 months pregnant. So when I finally got in to see the specialist he looked at me and said,"Oh you have ascites". My wife asked what was that and he explained that it was a sign of liver disease. He proceeded to ask me about my past and whether or not I had ever used intravenous drugs or whether or not I presently use drugs, such as sniffing cocaine through a straw. He also asked me do I drink alcohol and my answer was an emphatic "NO" to all of the above. So he probed some more. "What about tattoo's, what about Tylenol". I explained that I did have a tattoo and he questioned me as to how long ago I had gotten it done and where I got it done. My wife told him that I did take a lot of Tylenol. Even though all of the above answers to his questions were unequivocally "NO" he still asked to examine my arms for track marks. He had no bedside manners and treated my wife and I cruel. He scheduled me for a liver biopsy at Centra State Medical Center in Freehold and at this time I was using more of my sick time from the Post Office because I had plenty of it.

While awaiting the results of the biopsy, the doctor prescribed diuretics to remove the fluid from my abdomen. The drugs did work because my stomach went back to its normal size. I was still void and confused in the spirit and in deep denial over the medical report and even though the reports from my General Practitioner indicated that I was HIV negative and Hepatitis negative I questioned what could possibly be destroying my liver. I said to myself that it would go away in a few weeks and I would be as good as new. After all I was never sick a day in my life. I just wanted to resume my postal career, but not so fast!

The biopsy determined that I had portal hypertension in the liver and the good news was that the liver was cancer free. Now where do I go from here, back to work or straight to church? Neither one, I took my family to Disney World I just knew that Mickey Mouse would put a smile on my face after all that I went through. After returning from Disney World and doing further lab work, my wife, daughter and I visited the doctor's office for the results of the lab work. Nothing could have prepared us for the devastating news and even worse was the manner it was delivered! The doctor told us in the most callous way imaginable, "You have cirrhosis of the liver" and looked away. My wife began to cry and I looked at him in disbelief. "What are you saying, I do not understand"? He again repeated his bone chilling statement and stood up and told us that he was referring us to **UMDNJ**, University of Medicine and Dentistry, Sammy Davis Liver Center and the nurse would give us the necessary information we needed to contact them. My wife, child and I left the office and sat in the hallway lounge and cried in disbelief. My diagnosis was a hard pill to swallow because I did not know what they were talking about, but the doctor told me that in about 3 or 4 months," you'll know". So I went about my business as usual, not listening to a word that he had to say.

Then one day the disease jumped on me and I couldn't get up! In the meantime, I fired that doctor because he was nasty and disrespectful to my wife. He treated us like we were street people. I told him that I was the Manager of the Year in 2000 for the Post Office, but that did not hold any weight outside the P.O. These people did not give a damn about the job I held down. They thought that I was a black man who had destroyed my liver using alcohol or shooting drugs. All who knew me knew that was not the truth. They used to call me the doctor because I lived healthy. I used to sell Ginseng, Royal Jelly and all kinds of Natural Herbs. I thought I was healing folks with my Chinese Medicine but I was the one who now needed a healing. After spending months in and out of the clinic at UMDNJ my health began to rapidly decline. I began to lose more weight and I was also starting to lose hope. In my opinion, the UMDNJ liver Center was awful. At every visit it was overcrowded, unprofessional and they would tell me that I would live and they would see me on the next office visit. The ascites had returned, UMDNJ Liver Center was not treating my condition. No one was giving me answers and so one day, after several failed attempts with appointments that the hospital had scheduled for me to see doctors in preparation for me to get an organ, I stopped going to UMDNJ. I would often spend 4 or 5 hours during each visit and after becoming frustrated and my condition worsening, my wife finally decided to contact a new specialist.

Depression and denial had just begun to set in and I began to lose all hope and the enemy of my soul was aware of an opportunity, an opportunity to attack. Port holes were beginning to open, people were telling me that I was poisoned and the employees at the post office had slipped me a "Mickey" as payback for the years of my hard nosed supervision. I was disliked for years and there were those who did not want to see me climb the corporate ladder. It was often said that they "fixed" me with food and drink, which I often accepted, from co-workers. Being a man who was handicapped in the spirit, I allowed the enemy to attack. Take over was exactly what happened, I was now involved in tarot cart readings which opened more ports of evil worship. I became involved with wicked people all because I did not believe in the medical doctors diagnosis. I did not believe that Jesus was a healer or that God was my salvation, so I allowed people to perform exorcisms on me in an effort to heal my body. They would break eggs on my naked body and rub the contents over my torso. While chanting, they would then take the egg shells, yolks and egg whites, place them in a bag and dispose of it in a strange neighborhood supposedly, ridding me of the evil elements destroying my body. All of this was to no avail, so wouldn't you think I would cry out to the Lord now...wrong.

I continued exploring and relying on the witchcraft process. Now I am gathering sea water, 5 gallons to be exact. I was told to go to the sea and collect 5 gallons of sea water, take the water and drive over any bridge in the state, and remain on that side of the bridge for 2 hours before returning and taking a bath in the sea water along with 20 dollars worth of silver dimes. Yes, silver dimes, which had to be boiled in water for 30 minutes, dried with a white hankie, and then placed in the sea water. I was to soak in the water for 45 minutes in order to cure the evil inside my body. They say that silver kills werewolves; all that happened to me was a skin rash. To no avail, still sick in the body and handicapped in the spirit, what shall I do? Reeling now, constantly losing weight and hope for life, I continued to travel through darkness. Now I am recruiting individuals to help me carry out the devils plan. His plan is to destroy each and every one of us through various means, murder, sickness, adultery, and perversion just to name a few. Broken, I continue to press my way towards evil worship. But I did not even realize what I was getting myself involved with. Sickness was a new thing to me, I was never sick a day in my life. I have watched my loved ones suffer but never in a million years did I ever think it would happen to me. With all of my Marine Corps toughness and discipline and what I had endured in the Marines, still this illness had beaten me down.

I now find myself traveling to the Bronx, New York for witchcraft sessions. But first I had to pick up a Spanish interpreter in Union City. She knew the connection in the Bronx. There was something odd about the neighborhood and the house. It was the only one family house on the block and was surrounded by apartment buildings. When we pulled up to the house it looked eerie, the house was dark and it appeared unlived in. When we were welcomed into the house, I detected a foul scent. It was a burning smell, but not like a fire, one that I can't describe. A guy came in the room where they had me sitting. This room had shrunken heads in a jar and witchcraft paraphernalia all around and roaches were running up and down the walls. The first thing this guy said to me in English was "Pay Santa Claus". He wanted his payment before he got started. I paid the man his fee and he proceeded to move rocks around the table. He told me to pick up a rock while he chanted in Spanish. We did this for about an hour, and then he wrote out a prescription in Spanish. My interpreter translated it back to me. It stated for me to go and purchase 5 different kinds of fruits. At 7:00 a.m. I had to arise and repeat some words in Spanish that they taught me to say. This was also supposed to destroy the demon inside of me. The man did indicate to me that I was not poisoned at work and he could not explain what had caused the liver to become diseased.

Seven days passed and there were no positive results. The only thing that happened was that I became weaker and lost more weight. I had no appetite. All hope was gone with this witchcraft thing, as my bank account became depleted from sessions with these evildoers. I was in and out of Botanicas purchasing all types of oils to bathe in. What shall I do now? Well someone mentioned Holistic healings and medications, so I set out to try that. This one particular Holistic doctor swindled me out of hundreds of dollars. I spent hundreds of dollars getting infused. This particular doctor had me purchase all types of pills from him. He had changed my diet; he had me throw out all the food in my house. He said all the food I had eaten from birth had diseased my liver and that he could cure it. After a few months of this nonsense with him, he had become a thing of the past. Still void in the spirit and now broke in the wallet. When will I get better? When will help arrive? My wife wants me to go to church with her and I am constantly telling her "NO"!

Someone told me about another Holistic Doctor and that I should set up an appointment to go and see him. Now at this time I am not connected with any medical doctors, I have stop going to the UMDNJ Liver Center, I have given up on the witchcraft process and now I feel that I am starting to run out of time. This new Holistic Dr. was a good man. He tried to help me, he wasn't about the money. His only fault that I now find was that he did not want me to see any medical doctors while he was treating me. He told me that he was going to rebuild my liver and I believed him. I actually believed in him more than the medical doctors because they were talking about a transplant and medication for the rest of my life. This doctor did not practice witchcraft; I believed he was a spiritual man because he spoke of God all the time. But I did not want to hear any part of that conversation. I did not want to hear about God. He kept me going with his treatment and medications claiming that he would rebuild my liver. He would touch my body parts and he said they were responding back to him. I really believe he helped me with a lot of other medical problems that I had due to the disease. But he could not do anything with the liver. The liver is now breaking down rapidly and the ascites has returned and that meant that I would have to seek immediate medical attention.

The Holy Spirit has now led my wife to a great doctor in Red Bank. He was an expert in the field of gastroenterology. Oh he was such a nice guy. The whole staff was terrific, they took me under their wings, treated my ascites weekly with parasenthesis. This was a procedure where they would take what seemed to be a foot long needle and stick it in my lower abdomen to drain the excess fluid that accumulated in my outer belly. When they first started to drain my abdomen, they would extract at least 2 or 3 liters of fluid. Each liter bottle of fluid that they would extract would take a pound or two of weight off my body.

Early spring 2002, I now find myself constantly in and out of the Riverview Medical Center. My body is starting to go through some serious changes and besides the weekly parasenthesis I start to develop varices in the esophagus. The doctors had warned me that if one of these varices ruptured there was a possibility that I could bleed to death. My gastroenterologist and the staff had listed me as a number 1 priority. They knew the severity of the disease, which they constantly relayed to me but I chose to stay in a constant state of denial. Now I was finally forced to retire from the job that I loved so much and kept so close to my heart. Well I was so weak and mentally withdrawn that I really did not care. I decided that I wanted to die because I felt that my life was over now, after all my job was my life and all my power and self esteem had dwindled away.

Day in and day out I sat at home pondering over whether I would ever resume my career. Suddenly, one day as I was preparing to attend an evening event with my wife I felt a sudden urgency to vomit. I proceeded to the bathroom to vomit and I can remember my son yelling to my wife to get in the bathroom immediately. "He's bleeding mom, help him." It was surreal I didn't even realize what was happening. When I went to the toilet to vomit it was all blood, fresh red blood. My wife and kids freaked out as we rushed to the hospital I later found out that my varices had ruptured and it didn't look good. They performed emergency surgery that night to bandage the varices. I should have died that night because I lost so much blood and my blood pressure dipped down to 63/40. So low that they sent me packing to the critical care unit immediately following surgery. I managed to survive that round because God had a plan for my life that I was still unaware of. Even after being heavily sedated, I can still recall how my brother and his wife came in my room and prayed. They prayed so loudly that the nurses told them to be quiet.

Now my gastroenterologist connects me with Thomas Jefferson University that specializes in liver transplants because things are now out of his control. You see my doctor had graduated from Medical School there and he knew that they had a good liver center. He called and set me up for an appointment to get evaluated for a liver transplant. Now I am weighing about a hundred pounds soaking wet. People are starting to stare and question my health. A few of my neighbors made a few cold remarks. "What's wrong with your wife, she isn't cooking anymore?" and many different dumb things that people would say. One of my neighbors told me that before he found out that I was sick he told his wife to lock the windows and doors in the house he thought that I was a crack head because of my appearance. People would stare me down everywhere that I would go. I was emotionally crushed. I knew my appearance was horrible but it was confirmed when I went out in public. I became impotent but my wife did not care. She loved me despite my deteriorating health. I hadn't made love to my wife in the last 8 months and I was ashamed of my body and I couldn't even look in the mirror. My body began to go through more dramatic changes, just like the doctors had explained in the beginning of my diagnosis. I was only sleeping two or three hours a day and I became cachetic, as the disease destroyed my muscle mass. They told me that I would soon start to lose my mind and that depression would soon set in. They informed me that there was nothing they could do medically to save my liver and I find myself now in stage 2 of liver disease. As the medical doctors try to determine what has caused the liver to become diseased, I am holding on for dear life. They inform me that in order for me to survive I would need a liver transplant. They had also told me that 6 months ago at UMDNJ and I wasn't hearing it then and I wasn't hearing it now, I would rather die first before they experiment on me with someone else's organ. That talk about receiving a transplant led me to witchcraft and holistic healing to prevent such a thing, but it is becoming more evident that this is what I will need in order to live. There were times when I just felt like I was just dead! Just existing and waiting on an organ that I didn't even want. When people around me laughed at certain things I would become angry and just seeing people smile would make me so upset. I used to ask myself," why is the world going on as usual and I am here sick as I can be"? Watching this entire situation take place around me only made me feel more isolated and unhappy. My wife would cry so hard just seeing our neighbors enjoying life with their families while she prayed and cried and asked God to step in. Karen saw something that no one else could see as I carried a burden as heavy as the earth on my shoulders. Anger boiled inside me and made me wonder whether or not I was losing my mind, which in all actuality I was. My liver was no longer functioning properly; toxins were being trapped inside my body. In a state of mental confusion, I blamed myself for what I was feeling and lashed out at everyone around me. I would curse my wife daily and I existed in a cloud of anger and depression. I would tell her, "Just let me die". I told her that I hated her, all because she wanted her husband to survive and learn to call on the name of Jesus. But like so many others in the past who told me to call on the name, which is above every name, I failed to do so. I was mean to my children, sick in my mind with encephalopathy, sick in the body with liver disease. I just couldn't die quick enough! My blood pressure has now become unstable and I find myself repeatedly in and out of the hospital.

In the year 2002 I am hospitalized on what seems to be every major holiday. I can remember being discharged the morning of the 4th of July to only have to be readmitted later that same evening as the fireworks burst in the air. I spent more time in the hospital than I did out. In the meantime, down in Philadelphia they were continuing their pre-transplant evaluation to determine my placement on the transplant list.

While back in Jersey they were keeping me as comfortable as possible and monitoring my body's every change. But I didn't care I just wanted to die and die in a hurry! There were times when I would leave out of the house in the middle of the night because I could not sleep anymore. I believe I was sleeping about 4 hours a day just like the doctors had previously informed me, this would eventually occur as part of the symptoms of the disease. My wife and I would get physical as she tried to stop me from leaving out of the house in the middle of the night. There were times when she would flip me and man handle me to keep me from leaving. I was on a suicide mission, I would call her parents in the middle of the night and tell them that Karen was beating me and stopping me from leaving out of the house. Many times I would escape and drive up and down the Garden State Parkway almost crashing several times into other cars and the median because I was so weak and I could not control the vehicle. I never once thought about the stress I was putting on Karen and my loved ones. When I arrived home after these escapades she would be waiting at the door looking restless and stressed out because of my foolishness. Do you know how much stress I was causing my family? Where was I going? Straight to hell so I thought. Sometimes I would drive up to my father's house to awaken him out of his sleep, complain about how cruel Karen was to me, and leave out ten minutes later. Then I would travel to Karen's parents house tell them the same story and stay another 10 minutes. I was just causing hurt and anguish to all the loved ones that were supporting me. But these stories of her mistreatment towards me were not true. I was actually losing my mind and the liver disease was getting the best of me. Karen has now started to have vigils and prayer sessions at the house. She would invite family and close friends to the house. They would eat and pray while I lay in the bed motionless. They would pray and cry some more. After they would pray and cry I would hear laughter in other rooms of the house. This made me so angry, after all this was my pity party and there was no room for laughter. Karen is picking up my medicine from the holistic doctor because I am now losing my voice. She does not want me to get on the highway and travel because I am so weak. Yes I could no longer speak above a whisper because this disease had started to affect my vocal chords.

Great news from Thomas Jefferson Hospital had just come in. They stated that I had been placed on the transplant list and because of my rare blood type and my grave condition I was placed 5th on the list. This was nothing but God and I could not see it then. At this time they could not determine what had caused my liver to become diseased. I was not a drinker, I did not use IV drugs, and yes I did have a tattoo but it was determined that I was Hepatitis free as well as HIV and Cancer free. But through further testing and I mean to tell you that they test for everything they determine that I had cryptogenic cirrhosis of the liver. This means the origin of my liver disease was determined to be unknown. I was told that "crypto" meant from the grave and that really spooked me out. My so-called friends are now far and in-between. I must inform you that if you are sick more than 30 days, you will really find out who is in your corner. However, my family and close friends are still strong. All of my so called friends that used to frequent my home for cookouts, ballgames, super bowl parties and watch PPV fights had stayed away. It was the friends that I didn't spend much time with showed up and were there for me through thick and thin. Friends like BJ, Bert, Bashir, C.C., Amin and Koti. Phone calls were coming in from people who I thought didn't even care about me. The prayers of the righteous were going up from all over the world. June who is my best friend's wife is from Kenya, Africa. She had prayer warriors corresponding to us and praying for me all the way from across the Atlantic. I had a nephew who was stationed in Korea who also knew the Lord he was praying for me also. Prayers were coming in from the West Coast as far west as Hawaii. Family prayers from up and down the Eastern Seaboard but was I praying, "No". Still lying there waiting on death and for someone else to pray for me.

I recall sometime in May Karen insisted that I go with her to this early Morning Prayer service at her church. The name of the church was Second Baptist in Perth Amboy. I don't know what made me go but I went. This was the first time since my mother had passed away that I had been in a church. I walked into the sanctuary with the help of my wife because I could hardly walk at this time. So as we entered the sanctuary it seemed as if all eyes were on me. I must be honest that I looked so bad that I was just skin and bones. I was emaciated and caught the attention of many at the 5:30 a.m. prayer service. It seemed as if the service had stopped when I walked in. At the end of service the Pastor and his ministers, at the request of my wife, began to pray for me. I really didn't know what they were praying about because half of them prayed in tongue and the other half were laying hands on me. There was this one that they called the Bishop and I still to this day remember his eyes, he was seriously driven. He had the look in his eyes like my Senior Drill Instructor had back in the Marines. I knew this guy was for real. After they prayed for me and anointed me with Holy Oil they helped me back to our car. They told my wife that they were going to be there for me, no matter what! They asked me if we needed money for bills, food, or anything for the family. They were loveable people and they did not even know me. The Bishop said that he would call me and pray with me at home by way of the telephone. So as the prayers of the righteous continue, when will my blessings become evident? I guess no time soon. Bishop prayed for my wife to be sustained from the grief and burden that still lied ahead of her. He later told me that he did not think that I would survive because I looked so seriously ill to him. Bishop was a man of his word, he called me on the phone and he prayed with me and he even sent brothers to my home to check on me. They presented my family with an offering to cover our needs. With my low-pitched voice I asked my wife, "Why do they love me so much?" I was referring to the people from her church. She explained to me that this was a loving and caring church but I still did not understand. Now my wife has doubled the size of the vigils and prayer sessions. I am now seeing friends gather around my bedside that I have not seen in years. Cats that were not even close to me when I was running the streets as a "playa" back in the day. My brother would lead in prayer most of the time.

I finally started to listen to some of the prayers but I still did not want to live. I remember calling my brother one night about 2 or 3 in the morning telling him that I just wanted to die. My body was in pain and I was suffering. I am weighing only 95 pounds now. I couldn't even hold a glass of water in my hand. Now all of a sudden I am starting to lose control of my bodily functions sporadically. I was losing so much body fat that I began to lose my body temperature. Here it is early June and I can recall everyone dressed lightly and I was in winter clothes. Hats, coats, earmuffs, you name it I needed it, not to mention how foolish I looked but I was freezing and could not get warm. My body has started to become skeletal. Now I can't walk as much because I would easily become tired. I was now having anxiety attacks that landed me back in the hospital. While in the hospital the phone is constantly ringing because the days ahead do not look too promising. Time is starting to run out. I am starting to build a little confidence about this transplant, but I can still remember in the back of my mind what the holistic doctor told me, "Don't get a transplant because they do not work". At this time his word was God. So I went along with the medical doctors to buy me some time so that I could allow the holistic doctor to rebuild my liver. After all he said he had it functioning at 87% and there were times that I did feel better or so I thought. The reports from the medical experts indicated that a transplant was still the only thing that would save my life. I began to grow deeper into denial and saying to myself that maybe tomorrow it will all go away. Not hardly, the disease was beginning to progress rapidly. Now I am back in the medical center in ICU, all but dead. When a patient is placed in ICU for a long period of time they may develop ICU psychosis. I believe I experienced this because of the constant glare of lights 24 hours a day and the monitors beeping and blaring day in and day out. No windows, no television to divert my attention. I began hallucinating, hearing and seeing things that were not actually there. But there is something that is inside of me that just wouldn't let me die. Was it my mother's spirit? Could it have been my fighting marine spirit? Or possibly could it be God?

Knowing what I know now, it could not have been nothing but God. Yes my mother's spirit was inside of me and yes the marines taught me to endure the worst, but it was nothing but God that continued to give me life. As Elder and Deacon Barlow constantly pressed their way to the hospital to see me and pray for me, I wondered if I would ever learn to pray for myself. I would look forward to seeing them on Sunday's at my hospital bedside. I recall a time when they came in all dressed in their church whites. God was trying to send me a message, so when will I respond, and whom will I respond to. Only God knows. My family can't get through to me, Bishop is praying, the Barlow's are praying, it seemed as though the World was praying, but when will I pray for myself. Oh God, when will change come, when will joy come? Now I have spent the last 30 days in hospital and bedsores are starting to develop. I had one as large as a golf ball on my rectum. Oh, the pain and the discomfort that I was in. It seemed as if the hospital staff did not care. Some of the nurses were so cruel they didn't even want to touch me. They thought I had Aids and even if I did, no one should be treated the way that they treated me. I am beginning to lose control of my bowels. They did not change my diapers when they should have and they did not feed me properly. I could no longer use my limbs and I could not feed myself.

I requested they move me to another floor and after many complaints from my wife and myself they finally moved me to the 5th floor where I encountered Stella, a Health Care Provider who worked on that floor. She was a stocky built black woman. She was a no nonsense type of lady. But I didn't care because since death looked eminent for me, she didn't scare me. You know I didn't even speak to her, I would just watch her with my eyes. She would fuss at me and tell me what she expected from me, Stella was strong and mean and always fussing, "Tony this and Tony that!" She even told my wife that she wasn't going to take my junk. You see I had a reputation for telling nurses off. I would request for the nurses to do their job such as changing me when I would become soiled or wet and I was no joke when it came to that. I wanted my behind to be washed down properly in hot water using a special soap and then I wanted the nurses to powder me down because in my mind if I was going to die, I wanted to die clean. I would also buzz the nurse's desk every 10 minutes and that really became annoying. I even went as far as calling security to report that I was being beaten. Boy I really had a rap sheet and they placed me from floor to floor because they were not going to treat me poorly. The nurses hated me and I still remember how they used to treat me. They were so cruel, mean and nasty. Satan had strategically placed these demonic imps all around me. They were assigned to me because they smelled the odor of death on me. It was as if a vulture smelled the odor of death on its prey in the wilderness. I can remember their eyes, deep blue and empty. Their eyes allowed me to see into their souls, evil, empty and non-caring. So I thought Stella would be no different, even though she was a black woman, she appeared cold but in actuality, she was an angel from God. Stella was a part of the process and I didn't even know it.

Chapter 6

UNFOLDING OF THE MIRACLE

A week had passed and I was still not speaking to Stella. She was still coming in my room fussing at me and doing what she had to do and then she would leave. But on this one particular day something came over me and I spoke to her. She was in my room that morning taking my vitals and I said to her, "I know how Stella got her groove back". She looked at me and almost fainted. She said, "Tony, you do know how to talk". From that moment on we began to talk daily and a bond developed between the two of us. She told me how she inquired about my health from the doctors and they told her that I needed a life saving transplant. But before that she thought that I had Aids and was upset that no one informed her differently. So after she found out my diagnosis, she felt sorry for me and her whole demeanor had changed towards me. She also found out through my doctor that I had just lost my mother and I was a healthy man whom had never been sick beyond a cold, a day in my life. Stella told me that she had just recently lost her grandson, so both of our hearts needed healing. It was nothing but God that brought Stella and I together. Stella and I grew closer to one another and she became like a mother to me. I can recall the times when she would come into my room before she punched the clock to start work, just to kiss me and say "Good Morning". She took special care of me and she would spend her entire lunch period with me to make sure that I was comfortable. She would always make sure that I was fed properly. She would make sure that my health needs were in order. This was nothing but love that this woman had for me. It was her scent; I could just smell her a distance away. There was a special connection between us, something that God had put into place. She never tried to preach to me about church or God like everyone else did. She was there to comfort me until the next step and the next step will blow your mind. After my wife had witnessed what her husband had been through, in and out of the hospitals, loss of weight, loss of hope, close to death on a few occasions, seeing the ambulance come to the house two and three times a week, she too had become weak and Stella was there to lift her up too. Stella had become part of the family and not only Stella, but also my neighbor Elna, "Bunny" was there 24/7. When the ambulance and police came to my house to rescue me Bunny was there. Whether it was 10 am or 3 am. When Bunny saw the flashing red lights, she was there. No other neighbor was true like Bunny. This white woman in her mid sixties took excellent care of me and she was like a mother. God is really good because although I had lost my biological mother, God filled that void by placing these women in my life. I must also mention my mother-in-law. She was there, in the middle of it all. She cooked and babysat while my wife was with me in the hospital. She was there next to me holding my hand and telling me to pray but was I listening? "No". Back to Stella, I would hate to see her shift change and she would hate to leave. During her 10-hour shift, she would spend several hours with me to ensure my well being. I would cry when she would leave me because my attachment to her had grown so strong. I can recall one night at about 1:30 am; I called Stella from my hospital room. I told her that I needed her to come back to the hospital because I was having a bad night. Stella got out of her bed that night, caught a cab and stayed with me. I almost got Stella fired but I needed her and she knew it.

By now, I hated my wife. Karen wanted the best for me. She wanted me to live and I wanted to die. After all of her efforts and attempts to get me to give into Christ, failed. She had Bishop Hilliard call me several times. She had the Deacons and the Elders come to the hospital to pray with me. She held bedside vigils and had prayers extended on both sides of the globe, and all I did was curse her daily. I was so angry at her for making medical decisions on my behalf because the Encephalopathy had taken over my mind and Satan had my soul and the imps were all around me doing his will. I would tell my only hedge of protection, Karen, to get out of my hospital room. I would tell the doctors not to listen to her. I would tell them that I was the patient, not my wife. For me, death couldn't come quick enough. I was sick of Karen, I was sick of my children and I was sick of living and I reminded myself of that daily. Many nights I put the pillow over my face but I was too weak to take my own life.

I was discharged again from the hospital; this was a weekly occurrence because I had become somewhat of a professional patient. I was home again, living downstairs in Jihad's room because of my inability to walk up the steps to my own bedroom. I was wheeled from the garage to Jihad's room where I would remain for days. In between my hospital stays I would sneak to the holistic doctor's office. Bunny would drive and I would get some of the holistic healing and get advice on the holistic approach and why the holistic methods would rebuild my liver so that I would not need a transplant. That was fine with me, I told him to restore me. He told me that my liver was functioning at 87 percent now. He told me and Bunny that my wife and I needed a vacation and that if Thomas Jefferson ever called for the transplant not to answer the phone. He told me do not take an organ, transplants do not work. He said that if it were him, he would not get a transplant. That was all I needed to hear no God, no transplant. I followed his advice; I planned a cruise for my wife and I. My wife tried to discourage it but I had planned the cruise without her knowledge because this is what the doctor ordered. The cruise was scheduled for July 8th 2002. I was incapacitated, in a wheelchair unable to eat unable to walk but according to the doctor, this is what I needed. Karen did not agree, she wanted me to get the transplant. She saw something that no one else could see. It was approximately 5 am on July 8, 2002. Karen and I were preparing ourselves to catch an early morning flight. I told Karen not to answer the phone that morning because I was taking her on this cruise and even if they called from TJU, it would not prevent me from going. Suddenly the phone rang and without hesitation Karen looked at the caller ID she screamed with excitement that it was TJU she picked up the phone. She looked over at me and said, "They have a liver for you and we must get there immediately". She was so happy, she told me to take the phone and speak with him. It was one of the surgeons from TJU liver center telling me that there was a liver in. he described it as a perfect match. He said the condition of the liver was like a Lexus vehicle with low mileage. I told the surgeon with my squeaky voice that I was on my way to a funeral down South. He asked me whose funeral would you be attending? I said a lady close to me like a mother. He said if you don't get here in two hours it's going to be your funeral and I told him I'd pass on this organ, give it to someone else. I told the surgeon I'd grab the next one. He then told me that this opportunity might not happen again. I then hung up the phone. Karen called Bunny on the phone to tell her what had just transpired. Bunny had come over to give us a hand and reminded us what the holistic doctor had said and that was "don't take that liver". We went on the cruise anyway. I was so sick on that cruise I had to see the ships doctor almost every night. Karen was miserable, one hundred degree heat pushing me around in a wheel chair. I couldn't eat, I was cold, and I wore a red jacket the entire trip. I was freezing in 100-degree temperature. I had the nerve to bring along snorkeling gear. Oh yeah before I die I had to snorkel one more time. I was so weak and decrepit, I could recall that two-foot wave that knocked me to my knees. The sand and the heat wore me out and folks wouldn't help us. I fell several times and blood was everywhere. People would just look at me and frown their faces. They must have thought I had AIDS or Cancer and even if I did that was no way to treat a human being. I can remember not giving a sick or handicapped person the common courtesy of not even holding the door open for them. Now I'm handicapped and in need of assistance. Thank you Lord Jesus for humbling my spirit. Because now I know and I can tell you because going through what I went through, yes God saves his anointed. Just cry out to the Lord but in this text when will I? On the cruise ship the couple seated with us on the first night of dinner never returned to their assigned dinner seats for the duration of the cruise. They discriminated against me the entire length of the cruise because I was sick, and ugly and I had an odor of death on me. My facial expression wasn't far from death either so people stayed away from me. Being black didn't help the situation at all. We stayed in our cabin and suffered the entire cruise. I still didn't have an appetite, I still couldn't sleep and I was just miserable.

All I could hear was Karen saying as she cried," You should have taken that transplant; we shouldn't be here and look at you". She began to cry some more as she begged God for help. She simply said that she was tired of changing my diapers, the mental anguish, the suffering of her husband right in front of her own eyes. My God, my God what should we do? I'm now in my final stage of liver disease, my body is broken up, I have no faith and I turned down the organ in Philadelphia. I had lost all hope because they told me that they were kicking me off the transplant list, what should I do? Upon our return home Karen is now in Philadelphia pleading to the Pre-Transplant Director of TJU hospital liver center to place me back on the transplant list. After he hears her pleas and wipes away her tears he decides to place me back on the transplant list. God is really working this thing out. Karen gets a favor from God and the director. I am now leaning more towards getting a transplant the holistic approach is no longer working. I am just existing now, not even living time seems like it's going so slow.

The days are getting longer and the nights seem like weeks. I have lost track of time, days and my surroundings. If I was to go outside by myself I would probably get lost. Omar and Ish are coming around more they are helping Karen out in any way possible by taking care of the kids, doing hair, cooking meals. Omar was my support, he was hard on me. He would tell me that I wouldn't die on his watch. I remember they would spend nights with us to make sure everything was all right. Omar is like a brother to me, we go way back. I mean back to the 60's. This thing was personal to him, my illness. The devil killed his father years ago, he would say that the devil wouldn't kill another one of his family again. Ish also had just lost her mother. They were more serious about my health then I was. Ish who is Omar's girlfriend had volunteered to give me a piece of her liver even if it meant death to her but the medical doctors decided that I needed a whole liver not a partial. Ish was the perfect match too but this wasn't God's plan. I had some more suffering to do. Suffering should bring you closer to God but I was a hard nut to crack. Ish and Omar also provided humor to my soul; they had me laughing so hard one night about a Mary Mary joke while I was in Riverview hospital. I mean to tell you that they almost had me go into cardiac arrest. I felt as though if I laughed too hard I would die. This body was ready to go out to pasture but who said so, is that God talking or is that me? God has the last word and he wasn't finished with me so the devil couldn't kill me right now. I didn't know how much further I could endure the agony. My help had to come from somewhere and I felt that God was past due when sending me help. But it was right in front of me and I couldn't see it. I tried voodoo, I tried exorcisms, I tried the holistic approach, but when would I seek God for myself. Yes my family is praying and the church is praying it seems as though the world is praying but when will I cry out. I knew I was a good husband to my wife, I knew I was a good father to my children; I also knew I was a good son and a good neighbor. My selfishness towards God had brought me to my knees.

I still can remember that Saturday in mid July 2002 when Stella told me that she wanted me to talk to her daughter. At this particular time I was heavily sedated on Demerol. Stella's daughter Margaret had phoned me around 11 am that Saturday morning. She said to me "Hi my name is Margaret, I'm Stella's daughter". She asked me if she could come up to the hospital and pray for me, I said yes. Can't you see that was God moving me then to accept her invitation but I was still blind and I couldn't see it. As Margaret entered my room she turned to me and said, "Hello, my name is Margaret" she had in her hands the Holy Bible and a cassette player. She then inserted a gospel CD into the player and I said to myself, "Here goes another person trying to lead me to the Lord". In my distorted mind all I wanted to do was die. I was so angered that I wasn't dying quick enough, when would this pain and suffering end. I had already tried to asphyxiate myself with the pillow but I was just too weak physically. As soon as Margaret played that CD and she began to pray and worship I felt a strange occurrence-taking place. The Holy Spirit had just moved in my room. Margaret began to speak in tongue, she started putting oil on me, she oiled the doors, she put oil on the walls, and she oiled the entire room as she prayed and spoke in tongue, the Holy Spirit had just taken over and I was starting to feel better. The gospel music sounded so good, I had remembered in the past how I hated gospel music. I can recall the times when I was at the post office on Sunday's. I would come to work in the morning and the employees would be listening to gospel music. I used to tell them to shut it down. I would tell them that this music must go and that we were here to work and not to praise God, I was terrible. Lord please forgive me I didn't know any better. Margaret was an angel that God sent to me; she is one of the main reasons why I'm alive today. She was a vessel used by God, she was my bridge over troubled waters, and she helped me gain the faith of a mustard seed. Margaret's unselfishness to me and my family will be remembered for the rest of my days to come. It was Margaret who brought me closer to the Lord. It was

Margaret who washed my broken body down in holy oil. Margaret had become part of the family, for all those who had prayed for me their prayers were starting to work. Although my health was on a constant decline my spirit was being built. I wanted more of the word, I wanted more of the gospel music, I wanted more of the holy oil, and I started to join in on prayer with Margaret. Things were starting to change in the life of Anthony Calloway. I wanted God now. Margaret had asked me, do you want to live or die. She was tough on me, tough love and that's what I needed in the name of Jesus. In the past there were too many pity parties. Margaret changed all of that, she challenged me to read the bible, and she made me go for myself. Not only did she build me spiritually she took care of me medically. She would change my diapers, wash my back side I had no shame in her seeing me naked. My body was so emaciated; I didn't care who saw me. Self esteem was shot and my manhood was shot, just broke up but my sister didn't care. She would wipe my behind as if I was an infant. This phenomenal woman, a complete stranger, this was nothing but God. I believe all those who prayed for me, God heard their prayers but God wanted to hear from me. When God finally started to hear that squeaky voice of Anthony Calloway miracles started to unfold. Oh I was ready to receive God now so when Elder Barlow and Deacon Barlow from the Second Baptist church would come in and pray for me, I was now willing to accept them. They had sent word from Bishop Hilliard that the entire church family was praying for me and in God's time I would be healed. I do thank the Barlow's and you will always have a special place in my heart. You two were a bridge over troubled waters but even with all of this going on my health had fallen to an all time low. My blood pressure and body temperature were both below normal and encephalopathy was destroying my mind.

I can recall one night, as I lay in my hospital bed, I envisioned a patient bursting into my room, calling me a "nigger" all because I hallucinated that I had won a 30 day stay at the White House for predicting a half time score of a football game. He then ran back into his room and jumped out of the window, all I could hear was glass breaking and people screaming. This never actually happened, it was just the encephalopathy. That's how bad off I was. The medical staff had then informed my wife that there was nothing else they could do, medically. They told her that she needed to admit me into a nursing home and that it would be just a matter of time before the end would come. None of the incoming organs matched my blood type. Now at the end of July

2002, I was weighing 90 pounds soaking wet, couldn't walk couldn't talk, in diapers, and my mind was shot. But now I'm walking by faith and I believe I shall live and not die. I knew at this point no matter what the diagnosis, God could still step in and turn this thing around. I no longer wanted to see the holistic doctor who claimed he was rebuilding my liver through his holistic approach. I no longer wanted voodoo, all I wanted was Jesus. The Lord had just delivered me from all of my fears and I'm finally starting to realize that no one heals like Jesus and if I have any chance of surviving this I would need Jesus. My father can't help me, my wife cannot help me, Bishop Hilliard couldn't help me not even Margaret. I need the Lord my God, the Lord my healer, that's who I need. But when will he answer my prayers, after all I wasn't a faithful steward. When will God step in and save this sinner by the name of Anthony Calloway? In the past it was hard for me to talk positive about God yet it was so easy to talk about tasteless things. Out of all of the free gifts that we may receive in life, prayer is the greatest one.

I was admitted to the nursing home to live out my last days until an organ became available. I now find myself against all odds. The possibility of an organ transplant is now slim. I ask myself why didn't I take that first liver on July 8. I know that I might not get a second chance because the majority of patients in end stage liver disease, like me, don't even get one chance; never mind two. But I'm calling out to the Lord for another chance at life. I have taken out a new residency in this nursing home. This facility seemed to be so nice, it was like a country club, and I had a suite to myself, expensive furniture, big screen TV, DVD player, VCR the works. I said to myself this was better than that stuffy room at Riverview but the only thing that was wrong was that there was no Stella taking care of me. Since I just gained the faith of a mustard seed I knew God would see me through. Margaret often reminded me of the scripture Isaiah 54:17 that no weapon formed against me shall prosper but she explained that weapons would be formed. The staff was horrible, they mistreated me, they had me lie there for hours in my own waste; they wouldn't assist me in my personal hygiene. My insurance was being billed $600 a night for my stay there with those imps. However, there was a black woman by the name of Connie who took good care of me. Connie was an ex-marine, a "WM" as we called them back in the day. She was strong; I can remember the times when she would pick me up inside of the wheel chair and place me in the shower and scrub me down from head to toe. My body had this odor on me, the odor of death that would not wash away. Connie and Margaret would argue all the time about me. Margaret wanted to make sure that her brother was being taken care of with kindness and respect. But, if only Margaret and my family were there when Connie was off duty they would really have something to fight about. Those aides, "imps", would toss me around like a rag doll and they were so mean to me. Here it is in the middle of August and I'm freezing. I wore ear muffs, an over coat, and a wool hat on my head. These imps would take my huggy blanket off of me and turn the air conditioner on; while I froze they would giggle. Yes, I was an angry patient but no human being deserves being treated the way they treated me in that nursing home. Here I am, 43 years old, the youngest out of about 100 patients. They didn't care; they treated the senior citizens cruel also. My wife would catch them on several occasions mistreating the seniors.

I find myself living like a castaway, sick in my body, sick in my mind, just holding on with the little faith that I had just gained. Yes, I wanted to live now and I'm praying to God to work this thing out. I know God is hearing my prayers and hearing my pleas and I trust that he will work it out for me. I'd been through so much in such a short period of time. Do you know what is like to be sick continuously for 8 months in a row? But now I have finally prepared myself to walk by faith and believe that Jesus is the light of the world and he who follows him should not walk in darkness but have the light of life John 8:12. So whatever lies in the future for Anthony Calloway I know I must pray and press my way to the higher calling of Christ who lives in me. Can you believe that prayer and obtaining faith has changed my beliefs? So if God sees fit for me to pass on, I now know that he has a special place for me in heaven. Because now that I have accepted the Lord he will work it out for my own good, whether here on earth or in heaven. If He sees fit for me to leave this earth and to enter into heaven, I will be eager to see my mom and my sister. But as my eyes were now set on heaven my daughter Niya who was 4 years old at the time told me at my bed side that Helen (my mother) told her it was going to be alright and don't worry. Oh how God can speak through the mouth of babes. Oh Niya was a prayer warrior, she led prayer and she also saw things just like her mother that no one else could see. Thus far there was no word from TJU on an organ. Time seems to be running out and that's just what the news article read from the Asbury Park press referring to me. It stated that this young man (me), who has been placed at the top of the transplant list at TJU was in need of a life saving transplant and that my time was running out. But whose time is the writer referring to? Man's time or God's time? Now that I believe in the Lord I know that everything will be fine. As my family continued to press their way to the nursing home my Aunt Goodie would cry and not to mention, eat up all of my Hot Tamales that my frail body would crave. My uncle Allie would prepare me all kinds of dream meals that I would tell him to make for me and once he would make these meals I would hurt his feelings by telling him that they were nasty. I was hurting my loved ones feelings each and everyday. Satan is still trying to control my spirit. Margaret would find out these evil things that I had done and make me repent and ask God for forgiveness. I guess a part of my heart was still cold and bitter. I would tell my brother to leave and get out of my room, I would tell Jamaal that he smelled and I didn't want him around me. I was mean to my neighbor Bunny (Elna) and she loved me so much. I blamed it on the encephalopathy, it was really doing a job on me but I believe the devil was really doing a job on me. I knew that if I were to survive it would only be because of the grace, mercy and favor from God that was on my life.

Meanwhile, back on the ranch, the nay sayers were telling my wife to get ready to make funeral arrangements and gather up the insurance policy. Some of them were even whispering in her ear how much money she would obtain after my demise. Karen stood strong with her Biblical vows even after I told her time and time again to leave me and get on with her life. I could no longer function as the head of the household. I could no longer make love to my wife, I could no longer feed myself. I could no longer use any of my limbs and I frequently asked her what do you want with me? Through all of this I could remember the surgeon saying a liver transplant is like jumping out of a plane that's about to crash and if the parachute opens and you float down nicely you'll live happily ever after. But if the parachute doesn't open you can't get back up in the plane and even if you could it's about to crash anyway. I later found out that it was nothing but God that I didn't receive that liver on July 8; you will read further on in the text and will understand why I'm making this statement. Now getting back to the nursing home, Connie was a good sister. She took really good care of me. I still can remember that late August day when I was returning back to the nursing home with my aunt and uncle after a few hours of furlough I saw Connie cussing and arguing with one of the other nurses about them mistreating me on the night shift. Connie told that imp that she would rip out her spleen if she mistreated me again. God has really placed his angels all around us and we can't see it because most of us are caught up in the world and we can't even see how God is even moving right under our noses. So the very next day as I awakened to find out that Connie was let go.

It seems like satan was trying to cut off what God has in store for me but now I'm starting to pray for myself and I needed to because Stella was back at Riverview and Connie was fired. The aides were giving me hell and treating me cruel I cried all of the time just like a baby and my body began going back into a baby stage. My hair thinned out, I was always in a fetal position, and my anatomy had shriveled to child size. At one time the disease had swollen my feet from a size 10 to a size 12 three month afterwards I was wearing a size 7. I went from a 34" waist to a 27" waist. They fed me baby food out of a jar. I was so horrible looking. My teeth had grown out of my mouth or should I say my face had sunken in so far that it appeared that my teeth had grown. My wife and her girlfriend would enter my room and bust me, picking my big teeth. I was so embarrassed about my appearance and you know what was so astonishing is that so far I have constantly blaming the devil for trying to destroy my life and kill me like he has done so many in the past, who were close to me. But I seldom ask myself now in 2006, was this nothing but God who had brought me to my knees? You know

God can get your attention if he wants to. God is the manufacturer he created me and he is the author and finisher of my faith. Even though this nursing home was plush in furniture it lacked the spirit of the Lord. God probably didn't visit this place much, all the wickedness that went on there. As much as I reported these incidents to the authorities here and at Riverview nothing ever happened, they blamed it all on the encephalopathy. But one early morning Karen came in after she couldn't get in contact with me via my private phone line. She would always talk with me in the morning before she left for work. I informed Karen of the things they were doing to me and she decided she would find out for herself whether this was true or not. They would disconnect my phone, pull the huggy blanket off on me, turn off the heat in my room, and blast me with the AC. I would try to pull the fire alarm but fell out of my bed several times. They were using physical force against me for no reason. I was only 85 pounds; they would leave me on that cold floor and torment me with vulgarity. They used to ask me "what are you going to do now". I cried so hard while I was there. I had history from Riverview for trying to call security and pulling the fire alarm, I wasn't a fool, and I was trying to survive because these demons are trying to kill me before the disease does.

I recalled a time when they held me down in the pins and needles position and laughed in my face just so that I would cry and beg for mercy and this is the God's honest truth. That's why they fired Connie because she had exposed their wicked ways. But one night I resulted back to my Marine Corps training and I was ready for them. I knew they would be coming for me about midnight so I gathered my hand device that was made of metal and a trigger with a "grabby thing" at the end. This is what I used to grab things with because I had no strength in my hands. So I placed this device under my blanket and I waited for them to come in. "What's your problem now Mr. Calloway?" as this demon got in my face. I pulled that metal grabber from underneath my blankets and I began wailing her in her head and face. Shortly afterwards, about 5 or 6 aides jumped on me, cuffed me to the bed and wrote me up. When Karen came in that morning they were surprised and they were caught in the act of mistreating me. She went ballistic and told them to gather my belongings because she was taking me home. She finally realized that all the stories that I had told her about being mistreated were true. They told her that she would never be able to take care of me and that I would die. She said, "Well he's just going to die then, because I'm taking him home today, he will not spend another day or night in this place!" She yelled, "Get him ready now"! They were still trying to talk to her and convince her to keep me there, but they were just moving their mouths because she was not even listening to them. She was throwing things in my luggage and her eyes were so angry and at the same time so very sad. She apologized to me later that evening about not believing me and she cried to her mom, "They tried to kill him mommy, but God was watching over him." I was so glad to be out of that place and back home with my family. My wife was very angry that day. Karen loves me despite all of my issues.

I can recall my brother telling me that "this too shall pass" and "one day I'll walk in the park with my family again". I couldn't see it then. My brother went on to say, "God would never give you more than you could bear". He told me that I had "Mommy's genes, the fighting to survive gene" but at this time only God could save me. So on that Wednesday afternoon when my wife snatched me out of that nursing home I told myself that the end was near. I was so sick, weak and cold. I could no longer control any of my bodily functions. The odor of death was now more prevalent than ever. I had already been in diapers for well over a month and at this particular time my wife couldn't change them quickly enough. She would just have me lie there on a towel and let my feces run out of me. I hadn't eaten any solid food in over a month so I had no idea what was coming out of me. Finally the medical staff informed us that it was the lactalose. So while my wife attempted to make me as comfortable as possible, we were just holding on for what the doctors described as my last week of life. One doctor even told my wife that if an organ came in today or tomorrow that I was probably too sick and too weak to undergo a 14-16 hour operation. At hearing this, my wife's faith just grew stronger. She went into spiritual warfare.

In the meantime on this same Wednesday, August 28th, 2002, a tragedy had just occurred less than 45 minutes from my home. God pulled me through for the next couple of days and I started to feel a little better. I had been praying, my wife was reading scripture to me and I began to gain an appetite. I was craving grilled cheese, applesauce and a garlic pickle. I would suck the juice from the pickle and chew the grilled cheese and spit it out because I could not swallow. The applesauce went down smoothly. I was actually beginning to perk up a bit but I knew that my body was on its last stance.

It was Friday, August 30, and we had just received a visit from close friends of ours. My wife propped me up in a chair with cushions because my behind was so fragile. My wife always had fresh towels under me because at any moment I would lose control of my bowels. So while we were talking with these friends who came by to cheer me up, I had an episode. I was mortified and did not want to let my friends know what happened. I told my wife that I was tired and wanted to lie down. She tried to discourage me reminding me that I hadn't seen these friends in years. When I finally got her to agree to help me to bed, I told her what actually happened. She went back out to the living room and quietly told my friends what really happened. They left my house in tears. I looked over at my wife and she was in tears. She told me that day that she just couldn't take it anymore. This was the first time during the course of my illness, over the entire year and a half, that I heard my wife say that she could no longer handle it. God heard Karen loud and clear and the miracle was about to unfold.

Omar and Ish came by later that evening just to make sure everything was alright. They actually spent the night that evening, knowing that my wife was at an all time low and that I was in the final stages of liver disease. They wanted to help out and take some of the work load off Karen. They had heard that Margaret was there the previous evening, Thursday night. Karen called her at her job and asked for her assistance because I had taken a serious turn for the worse. My bowels had locked up on me. This happened in the past while I was a patient at Riverview so I knew the consequences of my bowels locking up. When the bowels are not able to discharge the toxins that build up in the body it looks for another way to be released. In the case of liver disease, these toxins travel to the brain and cause encephalopathy. Margaret knew exactly what to do because she once worked at a medical center as a nurse assistant. Margaret was so spirit filled; she prayed first and then proceeded to clear my rectum. I tell you, I wouldn't wish liver disease on my worst enemy. Omar and Ish were committed to my family and I. Ish took out her clippers and gave me a hair cut since I hadn't had one in such a long time. It actually felt like I was getting prepared for the electric chair between the haircut, my wife accommodating food cravings, and the visits from long lost friends. Ish was giving me a fade style haircut until the clippers died on us. She ended up leaving a ring around my head, this was the funniest thing. Here I am 79 pounds with sunken cheeks. I couldn't walk or talk, I'm in diapers with a half completed fade. So they put me down for the night while they stayed up to talk and pray.

Early Saturday morning on August 31st, I was awakened by conversation. Ish was telling Karen that she dreamed of her mother. Now keep in mind that her mother is deceased and she told Karen that when she dreams about her mother, something good is going to happen. As Ish and Omar left my home that Saturday morning they had no idea what was about to happen in the next 12 hours and neither did I. But before you read on, always remember, God has no respect of persons. What he is about to do for me, he would do for you, no matter what you're going through. At 9 am that morning, Karen begins to set up for a family visit and prayer that was planned for later that evening. I didn't know that she had called a few of my old partners from Newark to come down, she called Curtis (Muke) and June from Virginia and they said they would come up. My sister-in-law from Northern NJ showed up unannounced, which she never does. It was going to be great, everyone together, food and laughs but probably for the very last time. After all, the doctors told me that I only had about a week to live. As my family prepares for this gathering there is another family gathering together 45 minutes southwest from where I live. This family was seriously grieving because they just lost their sister on Wednesday, August 28th 2002; she was pronounced clinically brain dead on the very day I was being discharged from the nursing home. This family was coming together to grieve the loss of their 47-year-old sister but how would this tragedy affect me? My sister-in-law and my wife were cooking and cleaning while I was sitting up and being fed.

The phone rang at about 10:20 am and my wife answered. She said hello and the caller asked to speak with me. My wife asked who was calling and the caller replied, "this is the liver coordinator from Thomas Jefferson Hospital, may I speak with Anthony". My wife continued talking to her and she informed her that they were placing me on standby. But we heard this once before, so neither one of us became excited. There are a lot of determining factors when it comes to the selected recipient of a donated organ. Even though I was number one on the list in my region for my blood type and severity, it still could go to another individual based on the size of the organ and other medical factors (i.e. fever, infection in the body). It could possibly go to an individual who was placed either number three or eight on the list depending on the size of the organ and also the person's body size. My wife hung up the phone and continued preparing for our guests. This was supposed to be a surprise for me so my wife hurried back to what she was doing.

At 12pm the phone rang again, this time it was Curtis and June and they told my wife that they had already reached Baltimore and their estimated time of arrival was three hours. Curtis, my best friend since high school, had always told Karen that whenever a liver became available, he wanted Karen to call him because he wanted to be there. He also stated that there was no doubt in his mind that there would be a liver coming in with my name on it. I hadn't seen Curtis since April when he drove up to Philadelphia to see me in the hospital. I remember him calling me at least two or three times a week but I couldn't utter a word, instead I would just give the phone to Karen. At 2:19 pm the phone rings for a third time, my wife answered the phone. I can remember hearing a hello; a whimper and then she fainted. I heard my sister-in-law screaming at my wife, "Who is it Karen"? But I did not hear her answer. I did know what happened in the other room. I heard my sister-in-law pick up the phone and scream "who is this, who is this"? The voice on the other end told her that she needed to speak with Anthony or Anthony's wife. She stated that it was Thomas Jefferson Hospital and she could only speak with Anthony or Karen. Karen was too overwhelmed by what she had just heard so my sister-in-law brought the phone to me. Miraculously, I answered the phone in a strong voice. I was eager to find out what had caused such disruption in the other room. The voice on the other end told me that the person who was supposed to receive the liver is too sick to go through the operation. She told me that since I was next on the list, I need to report to the hospital immediately. We had two hours to get to the hospital. My sister-in-law went back to check on my wife and finally told her all the details. My wife came crawling back into the bedroom on her knees, crying. I told my wife to hurry up and get me washed up and ready. I wasn't going to let another liver pass me by; I had already made that mistake once. My wife and her sister began making calls. Karen called her father and asked him to take us to Philadelphia because neither she nor her sister was in any condition to drive. My wife was still making phone calls and at one point I told her to get dressed because there was no time to spare. I did not know that she had spoken to my friend Curtis and told him to meet us in Philadelphia because the hospital had called and the transplant would take place that day. The sequence of events was surreal as if it wasn't happening, like an out-of-body experience. Out of nowhere, my friend Glenn's wife appeared in my bedroom. She was there to tell me that Glenn and his son would be coming to help carry me to the car. Bonnie, Glenn's wife, suggested that we pray and for the first time I actually lead a group prayer. I read Psalms 18: The Lord is my rock, my fortress and my deliverer. My God is my rock, whom I take refuge

He is my shield and the horn of my salvation my stronghold I call to the Lord who is worthy to be praised. The cords of death had entangled me. The torrents of destruction to my body had overwhelmed me. The cords of the grave coiled around me, I could smell death and we now know that in all things God works for the good of those who love Him who have been called accordingly to His purpose.

God called me by name on August 31, 2002 and said "son, you shall live and not die" and Romans 8:31 says if God is for us who can be against us. My father-in-law arrived just as Glenn and his son were carrying me out of the house. They placed me meticulously in the front of the SUV and we began what seemed like an endless journey to Philadelphia. My father-in-law drove silently and remained focused on the road. I can remember asking him to turn on the heat because my body was so cold. Here it is one of the hottest days of the summer and I am asking for heat. My wife and father-in-law were sweating bullets as I shivered. The tension and fear ran high as the traffic came to a complete stop. At this point, time was ticking and we had less than an hour to make it to the hospital. The liver had already been out the donor's body for 12 hours and wouldn't be viable for much longer. With urgency, my wife called the State Police and requested an escort to help lead us through the traffic. They explained that if the traffic continued for another mile, they would come escort us off the highway and down the back roads. Incredibly, the traffic began to thin out and we were on our way. My wife informed the troopers that we could make it from here and we didn't need the escort anymore.

The Holy Spirit had come over me; I was ready, prepared to handle any challenge that was before me. I was finally beginning to understand what this was all about. The next thing I recall was the emergency room entrance sign in the front of Thomas Jefferson University Hospital. The time now is between the hours of 4:15 – 4:45 pm. Curtis, June and their children were at the hospital when we arrived. Curtis and my father-in-law removed me from the SUV and placed me in a wheelchair. Although I was cold and confused, I was ready for whatever God had in store for me. As they pushed me inside of the emergency room, I could hear my name being called over the loud speaker, "Anthony Calloway, O.R., immediately". The nurses began to take me through "in-processing". Curtis joined me in the small room that was adjacent to the ER. He stood by as the hospital staff began making an attempt to draw blood from me. They had trouble finding my veins and poked me several times before finally giving up. This was an important procedure; they needed to match the blood type before the operation could commence. They were required to draw 21 vials of blood before the transplant began. There was no time to waste; my name was still being blared over the loudspeaker. All of a sudden one nurse steps in and says "don't worry we will draw the blood in the OR instead". So they proceeded to check my vitals and do all the other necessary procedures that were required prior to the operation. Neither my temperature nor my blood pressure had been stable for months but in order to have this operation it needed to be.

Between the hours of 5:30 and 6 pm, the miracle started to unfold. My blood pressure was normal 120 over 80 and my body temperature was 98.7. I was not cold and this was nothing but God. They proceeded to take me for a chest x-ray to determine whether or not the new liver would actually fit inside of my body. I was so frail and weak; I wondered to myself whether or not my body would be able to endure this 14-16 hour operation. I reminded myself that God has the master plan and I am walking by faith now. As I lay there on that gurney waiting to be transported to the operating room I began to have flashbacks. One of the flashbacks was when I first met Margaret and gained the faith of a mustard seed. She read to me, Luke 17:11-19 about how Jesus traveled along the border between Samaria and Galilee and went into a village where there were 10 men who had Leprosy. They stood at a distance and called out in a loud voice Jesus, Master, have pity on us. When he saw them he said, go show yourselves to the priest and they went. They were cleansed. When one of the men realized he was healed he came back praising God in a loud voice. He threw himself at the feet of Jesus and thanked him. He was a Samaritan. Jesus asked for the other nine men who he had healed. He wanted to know why they had not returned to give praise to God. Then he said to that one foreigner," rise, rise and go, your faith has made you well". When Margaret read this scripture I told her that if God were to heal me and spare my life, I would be like that one Samaritan. I would speak of the goodness of the Lord for the rest of my life. The time now is approximately 6:05 pm and a black female who was the lead nurse appeared in the emergency room area where I was lying on a gurney. She seemed to be somewhat on edge as she urged the hospital staff to speed up the in processing, as the surgeons were waiting upstairs in the OR to conduct the surgery. At approximately 6:15 and 6:25, the medical staff, in a hurry, rolled me from the in-processing room to the elevator. Accompanied by my wife, Curtis and my father-in law, I was wearing a red Marine Corps cap on my head. My spirit had perked up and I felt like singing a song. I could not remember any of the songs from the gospel CD that Margaret had played for me at Riverview Hospital so I started singing an old Marine Corps "boot camp" fight song. Shortly thereafter the anesthesiologist entered to brief my wife and I on his roles and responsibilities during the surgery. I was also asked to sign a release form and other associated paper work but this was difficult for me to do as I could barely hold the ink pen, in fact I dropped it several times. I finally referred them to Karen and told her to sign for me. I was now at the point of no return; life or death awaited me behind those double doors. As I said my last goodbyes to Curtis, my father-in-law and kissed my wife goodbye I was injected with the anesthesia. My wife and my best friend Curtis provided the following recount.

Approximately between the hours of 8 – 8:15 pm, a male nurse appears in the waiting room area. It was said that he introduced himself to my wife, my father-in-law and Curtis and he advised them that the surgery was about to get underway. He informed them that he would return in a while to give them an update on the progress of the transplant.

The time now is between the hours of 9:15 – 9:30 pm and the male nurse appeared again reporting that the old liver had been removed. He went on to say that the old liver was in terrible condition and desperately needed to be removed. He went on to say that the transplant was going great thus far.

Approximately between the hours of 10:30 – 10:45 pm a different nurse appeared in the waiting area. This time it was a black woman who was assisting in the operation. As tension and fear accompanied with nervousness was running high, she informed my family that she was reaching the end of her shift. She advised them everything was going great with the transplant and she wished everyone a good night.

It is now exactly 12 midnight and it was Karen's birthday, September 1st. A male nurse came out of the OR and told them that the operation was over and that I was doing fine. He went on to say that the lead surgeon, Dr. Kayler, would be out shortly to debrief them on the transplant. The time now is approximately between the hours of 1- 1:15 am and Dr. Kayler appears in the waiting room. She begins to debrief my family on the operation and my condition. By this time other family members had arrived. Dr. Kayler began to express how successful the operation had been, or so she thought. She informed them that I was now in post-op care and that they would be able to see me in a few hours. I was told that everyone dropped to their knees and thanked God. What a birthday gift for my wife but the devil always wants to steal your joy. Shortly thereafter another doctor appeared and informed everyone that I was not out of the woods yet. He went on to explain that the next 72 hours would determine if I would live or die. This is the critical period after transplantation, the body can go into rejection at which time infection can set and this would be critical. My family's faith was strong so they didn't allow that comment to dampen their spirits. The revelation that my grandmother, at the age of 101, told me back in June of 2002 was now coming true. Back then Grandma came over to me as I sat in that wheelchair confused and broken, feeling like an outcast a black sheep, she then told me that she had been on the "mainline" with God and that everything was going to be alright.

The time now is between the hours of 4 – 4:15 am; Karen and her best friend Patty are told that they are allowed to come see me in CCU. As machines blare and beep, I am attached to the respirator. Eyes closed with my hands cuffed to the bed rails, I lie motionless. As my wife slowly approached my bedside she says that when she got close to me, she kissed me on the cheek and whispered that she loved me in my ear and my lips seemed to motion "I love you, too". She broke down crying and Patty escorted her out stating, "That it was time for us to leave".

Later that day the rest of my family came to the hospital. They each were allowed to visit with me for a limited time. They kept informing my family that I was not out of the woods. I supposed they did not want my family to get their hopes up. But they knew, by his stripes, that I was healed. Karen had described me lying there looking much better than I did just 12 hours prior. The Prednisone had actually blown my face back to its almost normal size. Karen went on to say that as she cried and prayed over me a teardrop had fallen from my eye.

Days went by and finally I reached a point where I was strong enough to open my eyes. My vision was distorted from the bright light. I thought I died and went to heaven. I heard multiple machines sounding off, beeping and buzzing. The next thing I recall was an Asian nurse coming towards me and I knew then that I was alive. It was a strange feeling because I couldn't feel my body. All I could feel was my head. I couldn't really speak and I was still somewhat incoherent but I knew I had survived the transplant. Believe it or not I was still angry. I started to become frustrated with the nurses who were trying to help me. Satan was still trying to beat me but I would not let him have the victory. After being upgraded to ICU my memory had faded or lapsed and here I am with feeding tubes in my nose. Unaware of my surroundings, I couldn't recall seeing my family. I couldn't remember the last time I saw my family. I was wondering where they were and why no one was checking on me. In actuality they were always there. I just didn't remember, but what I do remember is trying to pull those feeding tubes out of my nose and throat. I was becoming irate and that mean spirit had just returned. The nurses are doing their best trying to help me and I am resisting all of their help. The devil was refusing to let go of me! Soon after the feeding tubes were removed I developed ascites again, which meant that my body was still undergoing complications. Even though physically I appeared much better there were internal complications plaguing my body. At this time, the vast majority of transplant patients would be preparing to go home after 14-21 days of hospitalization. But not me, the doctors had scheduled me for additional tests. They told my wife that this sometimes could occur but that was not the only complication I suffered. I developed foot drop in my right foot. The neurologist explained that during the surgery there was a possibility that a nerve in my leg was severed causing the condition known as foot drop. I was not concerned so much with the foot drop at that particular time, I was just happy to be alive and amongst the living. Two weeks passed by and additional complications ensued. Jaundice just set in and my eyes had become yellow. This had become a serious concern for the medical staff, as they did not want to lose the new liver. They quickly determined that my bowel duct had narrowed and a procedure was needed to reopen it. Stints had to be placed in my bowel duct to keep them open. Shortly after that I had to begin physical therapy before I could be discharged from the hospital. I had to be fitted for an orthopedic shoe. It was now approaching the month of October and I was scheduled to do an interview with the Asbury Park Press, a local newspaper in my community. I remember telling that writer that I was ready to come home whenever God would allow me to. At this time I knew I was living for God. All of these procedures that I still had to face, the stint that needed to be inserted, therapy for the foot drop, and the possibility of more Parasenthesis for the Ascites that may return. The possibility that therapy would not correct the foot drop could leave me permanently handicapped, never being able to walk again without the use of a cane. I knew God was on my side as it is stated in Isaiah 43:2, "But when you pass through the waters, I will be with you" meaning my procedures. God was telling me even with all of that and some more, verse 43:2, "I will be with you and you will pass through the rivers they will not sweep over you. When you walk through the fire" (procedures, surgery, and hard times) "you will not be burned. The flames will not set you ablaze. For I am the Lord your God."

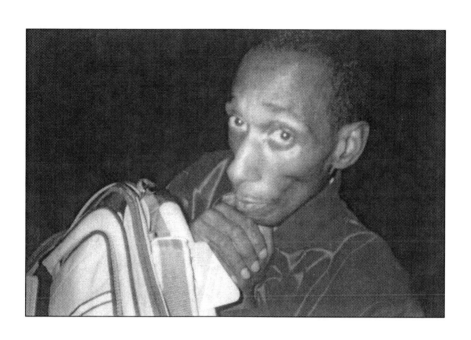

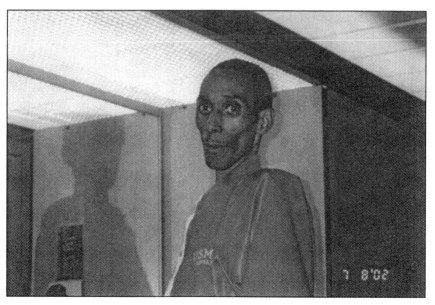

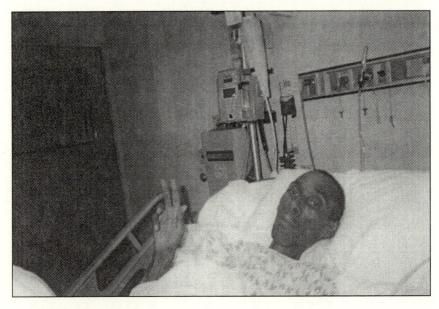

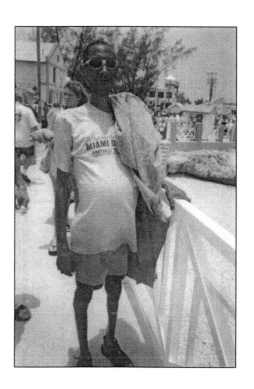

Chapter 7

The Long Road to Recovery

After a long three weeks I began to experience the ache of homesickness. I knew that I had told the Asbury Park Press reporter that I was ready to go home whenever God saw fit but I could not resist the post-op depression. I missed family members and my home. My family could not visit me daily; after all they were an hour and forty minutes away. I become somewhat lonely in Philly but God will connect you in the spirit with people you don't even know. There was a young black lady who was assigned to be my health care provider, her name was Matilda. She was in her mid twenties. Matilda was from Sierra Leone, Africa. Initially I did not take a liking to her because she never washed and changed my dressing the way I wanted her to. She also seemed to always have a ridiculing smile on her face. She was in awe at the sight of my body. Here it is three weeks after my surgery and I am still frail. As days went by Matilda began to hold conversations with me. I expressed my sense of loneliness to her because of the distance between me and my family. I explained that my family was only able to visit on the weekends. I needed support. The devil was still playing tricks on my mind. I still couldn't walk due to foot drop. The medication distribution was nonstop. I believe God moved her in closer to me, she became like a sister. We began to talk more frequently and my trust for her grew. With the approval of my wife, Matilda prepared home made meals for me. She was trying to fatten me up, to make me strong. She would spend her breaks with me to comfort me, she was a nice sister. God was forming a hedge of protection around me as Satan continued to move in closer and try to finish me off. I was convinced that God sent Matilda to me just like he had Stella, Margaret and Connie. These individuals were only in my life for a season but there was definitely a reason. When you have favor on your life from God, the Hell's fire cannot burn you.

Now it is time for physical therapy but being in a hospital bed for weeks had drained all of my energy. I had become somewhat complacent just lying there, handicapped in the body. When it was time for therapy I would come up with excuses but they had heard them all before. When I actually began physical therapy my bowels were weak and I would use the bathroom on myself during therapy. While weightlifting, I would try to lift the weights and my bowels would release themselves mid-lift. This was so embarrassing so dehumanizing. My self-esteem was shot but God placed in my spirit the will to go on. I started to rush my healing because I wanted to be strong again, independent. Now it was time for me to be fitted for my first pair of orthopedic shoes. First there was a pair that looked like a ski boot. It wasn't too bad; I had to wear them for about a month. The next pair had steel rods in the leg to support the foot drop. Somewhere around the first week of October 2002 I was finally preparing for discharge from Thomas Jefferson Hospital. The long road to recover lies ahead of me but first there were some special needs that had to be put in place. The hospital had to order special durable medical equipment to accommodate my needs. Items such as wheelchairs, walkers, canes, toilet padding and special devices for the bathtub. There was also a special pillow that had to be placed between my legs to prevent me from breaking my fragile bones or to avoid further nerve damage. To this day, I still place a pillow between my legs before I go to sleep.

Before I step foot out of the hospital I had to be assigned a physical therapist, occupational therapist, an RN and a home health aid to visit three times a week. But not so fast, just as I thought I was about to step out and go home there were questions as to whether or not I was able to sustain at home. I had not accomplished all that I should in physical therapy and the doctors thought that I could only attain those goals in a rehabilitation center. Doctor Kayler, one of my head surgeons, suggested that I go home because I needed home cooked meals and love. She knew I would not fair well in another nursing home or a rehab center due to my past experiences. God knew this first; He was not placing me back in the hands of the enemy. Everything went according to planned. Karen and her father picked me up that day. It was fall, the leaves were turning brown and the smell of coolness was in the air. I was so grateful to be back home in front of my big screen TV watching the game. I had all but forgotten about the long road to recovery that lies ahead. It was wonderful to see my family and my neighbors but I was not the same, life was not the same.

A death did occur on September 1st, 2002 and it was the old Anthony Calloway. Now a new spirit lived inside of me and I was coming to terms with my inner self. At first I could not grasp the reality of what I had just been through. My emotions became erratic and I would cry uncontrollably. Sometimes a simple hello would cause me to cry. I was so grateful to be alive. I was having trouble sleeping so I was given sleeping pills. Aside from taking an abundance of pills to stay alive, I was also taking a pill to control my depression. It had gotten so bad I began to refuse physical therapy and occupational therapy. The therapist seemed to be so hard on me, to the extent that I tried to avoid therapy at all costs. But I had to go through therapy in stages. Once my in-home therapy was complete I was to begin outpatient therapy services. I knew I had a long road ahead of me. My old life was a thing of the past, a distant memory. But, at this point I had lost faith. This road to recovery was just too overwhelming. When one therapist would leave another would show up at my house, it was constant. I didn't have the physical nor did I have the mental strength or will to continue my therapy. My will was broken. All the facts that I had been told ran through my mind and reminded me that my chances of surviving were slim. I was living with a compromised immune system and I was told that 80 to 85% of liver transplant patients survive the first year after transplantation. Only 70% live beyond five years. Believe it or not although God had spared my life and presented me with a liver, I didn't have the will to do what I needed to do to sustain. I was giving up again. Then someone told me to read Psalms 34:4 and 5. I sought the Lord, and he answered me. He delivered me from all my fears. Those who look to him are radiant. Their faces are never covered with shame. Just call on the Lord no matter what you're going through. When the poor man called and the Lord heard him he saved him out of all his troubles. I began to become more confident and to trust in the Lord. No matter what you're facing; liver disease, aids, cancer, broken home, broken relationship, can't find a job, whatever, God is not bound by our past. God can deliver you from all of your fears. If it had not been for God walking with me, by my side, where would I be? Satan the accuser of the brethren' will try to remind you of your past as he continued to do with me. What the devil meant for my destruction God turned it around for my good. Home therapy is coming to an end and outpatient treatment is soon to begin, and I am confident and have faith that I will persevere through this storm. Every week seven vials of blood were drawn from me. It was used to detect function of the liver and level of stress on the kidneys. I was taking weekly trips to Philadelphia to the liver clinic for post op evaluations. This was trying and exhausting.

Home therapy has now ended, thanks be to God, and outpatient therapy is about to begin. My wife has taken a leave of absence from her job to assist me during my recovery period. Professional therapists at school are counseling my children. Karen has started attending church again. She was keeping God close. She told me that members of the congregation at church were praying for my speedy recovery. Initially, going to outpatient therapy was difficult; I was still unable to drive. Karen had to get the kids off to school, get me dressed, down the stairs and into the car before she was able to drive me to and from my therapy sessions. As I continued taking my medication and making the weekly trips to Philadelphia, I also went to the lab for weekly blood work. I was finally beginning to see a light at the end of the tunnel.

I began receiving treatment at The Bayshore Rehabilitation Center. The staff was great. Many of them remembered me from six months prior when I first became ill. A few of the staff mentioned that they thought I had passed away. They told Karen that they remembered the last time they saw me in the late spring of 2002, I was emaciated and crippled. They were in awe to see that I was still alive. It was there that I regained my confidence, the staff constantly told me how good I looked. But physical therapy was difficult; I had to learn to do everything again. I started working out even harder; I even stayed there after my time was up. The staff mentioned to me that they now believe that all things are possible.

The time had arrived for me to begin seeing a neurologist for the foot drop. I can recall the times when he would inject needles into my leg in an effort to stimulate the shattered nerves. His first diagnosis was that I had lost enzymes in the brain that control the nerves in my foot. He claimed it was due to my chronic illness but further blood work determined that this was not the case. The paralysis was isolated to my lower right leg and foot. He prescribed medication and more physical therapy. He later explained that nerves do not regenerate themselves and there was a possibility that I would never walk again without the use of a cane or orthopedic shoes. I was just happy and grateful to be alive so the foot drop did not bother me. So with my foot drop, I continued to press my way through physical therapy. I actually started to get into the groove of working out. It reminded me of the old times before my illness. It was difficult for me to adjust to my foot being dropped. Whenever I tried to walk, I would trip over my feet. I remember one evening my wife had prepared a nice dinner for me and I wanted to serve myself because I was becoming more independent. So as I got up out of the bed, and headed to the kitchen to make myself a plate of food. Since my appetite was increasing I piled my plate high. I proceeded to take a step back towards the table to get started on my dinner but I forgot about the dropped foot. I tripped over my right foot and fell to the floor. Food splattered everywhere and I was humiliated. My wife screamed and was prepared to call 911. Although I ended up with a broken toe, we were able to laugh about that later. The enemy continues to attack me by playing tricks on my mind. I was starting to wonder if I would ever be able to run again and do all the things that I was able to do before my illness. I was a very active young man, I played football and snorkeled and at the age of 42 I believed I was still in my prime. I was just wondering if I'd ever be able to shoot hoops again, would I ever be able to walk again without all these devices. As the enemy continues to nibble at me like Jack Frost who nibbles at your toes during the winter months. I must continue to pray and speak healing with my tongue. As I now start to excel in physical therapy, my therapists were pleased with my motivation and progress. There was so much I had to accomplish, I needed to learn how to dress myself, prepare my own meals, I even had to learn how to drive again. My year and a half of illness had taken a toll on me. It seemed like post op was more difficult to tolerate than my pre op. At least during pre op everyone took care of me and my needs. Now I needed to learn how to take care of myself. Winter is now upon us and we are approaching the holiday season. Christmas is right around the corner and I had learned to do so much on my own, thanks be to God. My wife wants me to join the church with her now but I continue making excuses. After all the Lord has done for me, giving me a second chance at life, delivering me from all my fears. Why was I so reluctant to go to church? I felt that my appearance was not up to par. I hated the orthopedic shoes that I had to wear as a result of the foot drop. The shoes had bars attached that ran up the side of my legs. I was walking with a cane as if I was an elderly man, I did not want to be seen like this. My pride was holding me back but eventually I gave in anyway. I can recall the first time I went to church after my transplant still frail in structure but strong in the spirit. The Second Baptist Church in Perth Amboy had just changed its name to The Cathedral International and it felt so good to be in the house of the Lord. Some of the saints who remembered me from when my wife had first brought me to church came over to greet me and express how much they had prayed and fasted for me. A few expressed that I was a miracle from God and that Jesus Christ was still in the healing business. As my spirit gets a boost from being in service for the first time since early spring 2002, I asked my wife if we could come back the following week. For the first time in my life I wanted to attend church more. Having a compromised immune system my doctors discouraged over exposure in public places. I did not like having to wear a mask every time I went out in public. This was a critical time in the healing process so the slightest infection or germ could affect my new liver causing possible rejection.

My wife had planned a big Christmas dinner at the house for the entire family and close friends. This was the best Christmas that I ever had. For the first time in my life it was not about the gifts that we exchanged or the food and fun, it was about family and having life and being so grateful to God. January 2003, my weekly visits to TJU clinical have now become bi-weekly visits, as did my lab visits. My long road to recovery has finally come to an end, but not so fast. Late February I began developing ascites again. After numerous ultrasounds it was determined that my Vena Cava, the artery that carries blood from the heart to the liver, had narrowed. This was an extremely critical situation because the new organ was not getting the proper blood supply. There was a possibility of liver failure so I was once again hospitalized.

I wondered when my medical problems would come to an end. I was hospitalized for two weeks while the surgeons had to put stints (chicken wire stints) to expand the Vena Cava. I was prescribed blood thinners. The enemy of my soul just wouldn't stop, he wanted me dead but I have the victory and no weapon formed against me shall prosper. At this time I did not cry or feel sorry for myself, I just wanted to be home with my family. I was tired of going in and out of the hospital. Doctor Kayler treated the ascites and my abdomen was back to normal. I was ready for discharge and hear comes the enemy again. Not so fast Mr. Calloway, announced one doctor. He told me that the CAT scan revealed a blood clot and that my discharge would be delayed for at least another week. The medical staff was concerned that the blood clot would travel to my heart. I pleaded for the hospital to release me and admit me to a hospital closer to my home in the state of New Jersey. My family and I prayed and asked God to step in and turn the situation around. After days of treatment with the blood thinners my blood levels were finally acceptable so an MRI was scheduled. The MRI would detect whether or not the clot had moved or dissolved. Prayer is the answer to all your problems because when the results came back there was no more blood clot. The Lord my God had stepped in one more time and turned this thing around. I could finally go home and all I had to take was a 325 mg aspirin, rather than the stronger blood thinners prescribed earlier. This is a blessing because people on Coumadin are subject to heavy bleeding.

The enemy of our souls will try anything in an attempt to destroy us and he was trying to destroy me through my health. What shall we do against such an enemy? In the book of Ephesians 6:13, the bible tells us to stand firm, stay alert, and pray in the spirit on all occasions. So this is what I must do to defeat the enemy. Greater is he who is in you than he who is in the world First John 4:4. I must now confess my healing and fight the spiritual warfare that all of us are up against. After these procedures were complete, I was released from TJU for the last time besides my clinic appointments.

Chapter 8

Second Chance at Life

My health had improved tremendously, no further setbacks with the organ. The extremely long road to recovery is now a thing of the past. The revelation that this too shall pass is finally starting to take shape and I am blessed to be alive. In spite of my foot drop, in spite of my many medications, in spite of what lies ahead of me; God is still good. From my heart I just want to say thank you Lord for what you have done for me. Now I find myself adjusting to being home alone, without a career and without my sporting activities. My depression is now starting to progress. I find myself addicted to sleeping pills. Karen argued with me daily about taking them. She wanted me to try to get to sleep on my own. It was just so much easier for me to take a pill and sleep through my depression. The antidepressant drugs had dried up all of my emotions. Shortly after my transplant I, would cry over everything, now I can't shed a tear. I am back to being bitter and emotionless. Karen is becoming more and more concerned with my emotional well being. She contacted the doctors at TJU. They suggested that she wean me off the antidepressants as well as the sleeping pills but my wife took it a step further. She knew it was time for me to get back into church and that is exactly what I did. At the end of every service the pastor would announce the benediction. Karen would nudge me and tell me go ahead and join the church and accept Christ as my savior. But I was not ready. Although I had been reading the scriptures and had a personal relationship with God, I was still not ready to go to the altar. My wife finally understood this and she stopped pressuring me. On one particular Sunday the spirit had arrested me and I was ready to join the church and publicly accept Jesus Christ as my Lord and savior. Elder Barlow walked up to me and took my hand and walked me to the altar. Bishop Hilliard was preaching that Sunday and as he went to shake my hand and welcome me he looked into my eyes and said don't I know you. I said yes. He asked me my name and I said, "Calloway, the liver guy". Bishop went on to praise God for me being alive. Now I find myself going to church on a regular basis, every Sunday. My faith had become stronger. I realized that my weeping was only for a moment and joy did come in the morning. We are so impatient when it comes to God answering our prayers. God's time is not our time. I am a living witness to how my prayers and the prayers of the righteous were answered. A year and a half after my diagnosis and my illness, I am alive. I now find myself reading a lot of scriptures, I really enjoy reading psalms because it increases my level of praise. I moved on to proverbs and gained wisdom that I never had before. So as my praises went up my blessing were coming down. One day as I rose from bed and put my feet on the floor my foot drop was miraculously gone. God had just worked another miracle in my life. Although the foot drop was gone, I did still feel a tingling sensation in my leg. I still feel it to this day but I am not complaining. The foot was healed; the paralysis had just left my body, nothing but God. So as I rejoice in the Lord, my foot becomes stronger. I did not need the orthopedic shoe anymore; I got rid of the cane and began to walk. I couldn't wait to go outside to see if I could run. But first I must be honest; I was a little gimpy, unable to get my balance together. I was a bit nervous because I didn't want to hurt myself. After a few days of getting my balance and step together, I was back to my normal self.

Early March 2003, I was approached by the director of the TJU post-op liver transplant program about doing an interview for the Philadelphia Inquirer. I had no idea what the interview would be about but I was so honored to be asked that I accepted the offer without knowing. When the Inquirer contacted me I was finally given the specifics of the interview. I was told that there were deaths on the operating table. There was a mystery at Jefferson, 52 surgeries and nine deaths, which made for an inordinately high death rate. It was all about the span from fall 2001 to spring 2002 when eight liver transplant patients died in the operating room and the ninth died within hours of surgery. The Inquirer asked if I was aware of this but I was not. They went on to ask why I chose Jefferson as opposed to any other hospital in the area. I told them that my Gastroenterologist referred me to the hospital because he knew they had a wonderful liver center. I wondered if it was nothing but God who stopped me from getting that liver transplant on July 8, 2002. TJU has a wonderful transplant program and that is what I explained to the interviewer. I really can't explain what happened to the patients who died while undergoing surgery for their life saving transplants but I do know that God is the judge. Roger Jenkins who at the time was the head of the liver transplant program at Lahey clinic in Massachusetts, summed it up by saying, "the number of deaths at Jefferson seemed high" but he pointed out "they have gotten some other critical patients through, so they were obviously doing something right".[1] The article in the Inquirer went on to explain that I, a 43-year-old postal worker who had developed Cirrhosis of the liver, was one of the success stories. The article also explained that at the time of my transplant I weighed only 79 pounds and was told that I had a 50/50 chance of survival. Figuring I was dead either way, I took the chance and was grateful that at least they tried to help me. It is tremendous what they do down there. To this day I am grateful to TJU so I volunteer my time to the liver program by supporting and conversing with patient's pre and post transplant.

Easter is now a few weeks away and the Holy Spirit has arrested my attention once again to now get baptized as an adult. This will be my third baptism. I was baptized as a Baptist when I was a child, then years later I became Catholic and was baptized again. But now on Good Friday 2003, I will be baptized, as an adult on my own will. I will be cleansed of my past sins and become a new creature in Christ. Bishop Hilliard performed the baptism and before he sub-

---

[1] Philadelphia Inquirer, (June 1, 2003)

mersed me in water he reminded me that he could have been burying me seven months ago. Despite all this, there was still a void in my life. I was unhappy sitting at home. I wanted to get involved in the community; I wanted to help make a difference in someone's life. So one day while I was visiting my dad in the hospital I came upon an NJ Sharing Network Organ and Tissue donation information booth. I stopped to talk with a few of the people who were manning the information table. I explained to them that I had just received an organ several months ago. A few of them expressed how they had also received an organ so we began to converse for a while. After hearing their testimonies I began to gain confidence about my transplant. They had been transplanted years before me but you would have never known this unless they told you. I asked how I could join the NJ Sharing Network and volunteer to do donor awareness. They invited me to the next meeting where I met several more organ donor recipients. It was on that day in May 2003 that I joined the Sharing Network.

I was excited and anxious to be getting involved with something that touched me personally. I couldn't wait to do a donor awareness booth and speak about the importance organ donation. I wanted to make the public aware of organ donation. I believed I had just found my niche; I was tired of sitting at home. I wanted to become involved in community outreach and what a better way. I became fully committed to the Sharing Network and I found myself doing speaking engagements. I even had the privilege to speak before pre-med students at Rutgers University Medical School. I spoke at several venues from ball games to radio stations and I shared my testimony throughout the state of New Jersey.

There was still something inside of me that was unsatisfied. Despite my successful operation, the ability to make the public more aware of organ donation and meeting several donor families, I felt incomplete.

As my health improved I thought back to where I was in June of 2001 when I was first diagnosed with liver disease. I thought to myself at that time, a year ago, I was in Disney World with my family; reeling from the diagnosis and the possibilities of what could lie ahead of me. I wanted to take my family back so that we could enjoy Disney World as a family, so my wife and I began to plan. Oh, what a difference a year makes. It is now August, almost a year since my transplant and my wife, the kids and I are back at Disney to kill an internal demon.

Once we returned from Disney I contacted my transplant coordinator who suggested that we write a letter to the donor family on my one-year anniversary. My wife and I wrote the letter and forwarded it to the Gift of Life in an effort to find my donor family. In our letter we expressed our sympathy for their loss and told them how much their gift of life was appreciated. At this point there was nothing left to do but wait? I am still not feeling whole. Just writing that letter was not enough. The anticipation was overwhelming, I needed to hear something. I yearned to speak to this family. I took matters into my own hands and contacted the Oprah Winfrey show. I gave all of the specifics on what transpired and asked for their help in contacting my donor family. I also explained that I would like to appear on the show to talk about organ donation and my personal experience with having no faith and then gaining faith and receiving a blessing. I wanted the nation to know that God could step in and turn your situation around no matter what it is. The Oprah Winfrey show responded back by telling me that they were overwhelmed with requests and that my offer could not be accommodated at that time. I became disheartened because I had watched so many talk shows that lacked substance and didn't provide awareness, but my fight did not die. I went on to contact the Montel Williams show that also contacted me back. The Montel show took my information and told me that they would help me out. Unfortunately,

I never heard from them again. I was on my own. That is the problem right there, we're always seeking man to help us out. I should have known better. All I had to do was call on the Lord because he can make a way out of no way. So as my wife and I pray and ask God to lead us to the donor family, we knew one day our prayers would be answered.

As I continue to travel across the state volunteering my time for the NJ Sharing Network, I was asked to do a speaking engagement for a donor memorial service, which would be held at the Sheraton Hotel. This memorial was in honor of the families who donated their loved ones organs in the year of 2002. When I read the invitation it requested that my speech be scripted. Now as long as I had been speaking for the Sharing Network, I had never done a scripted speech. It was never required. But for this event, they wanted the speech to be prepared for me. I became a little annoyed after reading what they wanted me to say. I discussed this with my wife and chose not to speak at this event. After all that I had gone through, I couldn't imagine not giving thanks and honor to God before my speech began. But this was not the format of their speech. Little did the Sharing Network know that I was just not going to show up. That Sunday morning my wife and I went to church and I heard a fresh word from the pulpit. I believe Bishop was preaching that Sunday. The Holy Ghost had arrested my attention once again and told me to attend the memorial service that was slated for later on that day. So my wife, the kids and I went. By the time I reached the Sheraton Hotel I knew what I had to say but I needed a special anointing on my lips. In all of my experience with speaking, I had never needed to address grieving donor families. The hotel was packed so I was a little nervous. Upon entering, my family and I received programs and name tags that identified us as donor recipients or donor families. The Sharing Network staff had done a stellar job in organizing this event. As I browse through the program I noticed that there would be two speakers beside myself. One was a tissue recipient and the other was a donor family member. After hearing from the tissue recipient it was now my turn to speak. I said a quick prayer before leaving my seat. I asked God to anoint my lips of clay and bring forth the appropriate words to say to the bereaved families before me. I started out by first giving honor to God. I shared my testimony on my illness and how grateful I was to have received the precious gift of life from the donor family. I concluded my speech and was honored with a round of applause. Shortly after the testimonies were given it was time for the candle lighting ceremony. Reverend Dr. George Blackwell lit the first candle in the room and each person lit their candle from someone else. It was now time for my daughter to light my candle, as I was last in the row. My candle's wick touched my daughters and my candle was lit. Suddenly, this woman came over to where I was seated and blew out my candle. She then relit my candle with hers. I can't completely remember but she muttered a few words and then either kissed me or patted me on my cheek. I didn't really hear what she said because music was playing and people were crying. As the event came to an end everyone gathered in small groups or went over to view the quilts with pictures of their loved ones on them. At this time my family was on one side of the room and I was on the other talking. All of a sudden I looked over and see my wife engaged in conversation with a white family. She was crying so I became alarmed. I immediately rushed over to find out what had happened. My wife told me in a frantic voice that the family she was standing with was my donor family. God had done it again. It was another miracle in my life. After all, Oprah couldn't deliver, Montel couldn't deliver, even the Gift of Life couldn't but the Lord my God has delivered my donor family to me. I almost fainted on the spot. We all embraced and cried together. We proceeded over to the wall as a family to view the picture of my donor displayed on the donor quilt. This was nothing but God, nothing but a miracle. My donor family had actually received the letter from the Gift of Life a week prior to the event. They actually had the letter with them and showed it to us to confirm that they were the family. My donor family went on to say that they came in great expectation, even though they knew that this event was not designed to bring recipients and donor families together. It was designed to pay homage to the families of the loved ones who donated their organs. They had a feeling that day that something supernatural was going to happen. The donor family said that when they saw that one of the speakers was a liver recipient they wondered if I could be the guy with their loved ones organ. One family member told the rest, "never in a million years". But God had already arranged this special meeting place for us that day. My donor family went on to say that they weren't even going to come to the event that day because they were still grieving. They did indicate to us that they had planned on contacting the Gift of Life to assist in coordinating a meeting. God had his own plan.

Since that day, October 26, 2003, we are one. My donor family and my family visit each other and talk to each other. The tragedy that occurred back in 2002 that I spoke about previously was their loving sister Caroline. Her liver now lives inside of me. What is so amazing about this story is that her liver traveled from New Jersey to Philadelphia. The Sharing Network recovered the organ and transported it to the Gift of Life in Philadelphia, where I was listed. My donor family lives less than 45 minutes from my home. So now my life had come full circle. My health had finally improved, I had become a member at the Cathedral and I met my donor family. What is next in the life of Anthony Calloway? I started reading newspaper articles about young children who were being abused and neglected and that there was a need for big brothers and mentors. I am ready to focus some of my time to the troubled children and their families in my county. Somebody has to make a change and that somebody has to be me. The Lord led me to the Youth Advocate Program, an agency that helps troubled youths and their families. It's a job where most adults wouldn't dare bother. Who wants to deal with other people's troubled kids? The nay sayers were busy telling me that I was a fool and asking me why I would want to take on the behavioral problems of others. But this is the path that God wants me to walk for this season. The majority of my adulthood was spent on my career at the post office and I did not have time for the community. I didn't even have time for my own children. So I now believe that God is using me in this season of my life to help these troubled families. There is now a plea at church for the members to join different types of ministries. As I pray and ask the Lord to lead me to the right ministry I was lead to join the FOJ (Fruit of Jesus Ministry). Since I have a security background from the military, I felt that I would be a blessing to the ministry. Now I find myself involved with the NJ Sharing Network, Youth Advocate Program, and FOJ Security Ministry and believe it or not I still sense a void in my life. I felt like I needed to do more, I needed to be more involved in community outreach. After all I was given a "second chance at life", I just felt that I had to give back to society. Even after my doctors advised me that I could no longer participate in sporting activities that involved physical contact; such as football, the sport I loved most, I still had to find a way to get back on the field. So I took the state exam and became a certified high school track and field referee. It really felt great to be back on the field but this was not enough. I wanted to take it a step further, I wanted to coach. I began coaching little league soccer. God has really changed my priorities in life. He has also humbled my spirit. You know, God wants us to have a contrite spirit, a spirit without arrogance and self- centeredness.

The type of spirit I used to possess. God will allow trials to test our faith, as He did in my case. Our trials should draw us closer to Him.

I can still remember that night when Bishop Eddie Long was a guest speaker at the Cathedral. He preached into my spirit that all the suffering we have endured and all the trials and tribulations we overcome was not meant for us. That anointing was meant for someone else so that we could stand witness to God's grace and mercy and be an inspiration to someone else. He made me realize that this liver wasn't about me. It was about other people who were going through it and now I can bare witness to them. God is really directing my life. He has removed my shackles and now I am living free. I am no longer living for the world I am living for God's purpose in me. I am not my own, I belong to God. I am just walking by faith and trying to be obedient to God. There are times when I am awakened in the middle of the night and God speaks to me. I know that I am living from season to season and whatever God's plans are for me on Earth, I am ready to receive them. God has turned my mornings into dancing. What are your expectations from God? We receive not because we ask not.

I am now led to visit and minister to the sick, broken and bereaved. I do believe that I am fulfilling my purpose. I have done so much with my second chance at life. I am pleased to be walking this path. One Sunday morning in the spring of 2006 as my family and I left church, a woman approached me and asked to speak with me for a moment. She introduced herself and I did as well, but she told me that she knew who I was. She went on to say that she heard my testimony during church one day and she knew that I had received a transplant and that God had performed a miracle in me. She then escorted me over to her friend who I greeted. I noticed that she seemed a bit weary as though her spirit was broken. The woman went on to say that her son was in desperate need of a kidney transplant. She told me that she was the perfect match. Initially, I felt overjoyed because it was a blessing that he had found a compatible match. I was thinking that she probably just wanted to talk about the transplant procedure. But she then went on to tell me that her son had lost faith and was not doing well physically or spiritually. As a result, he was not in condition to receive a transplant. She asked me if I wouldn't mind talking to her son and giving him some inspiration on the healing power of our Lord and Savior. I agreed and we exchanged phone numbers. Afterwards, I introduced her to my wife so that she could be uplifted and supported by my wife's testimony. Both my wife and I spoke with her on several occasions, reassuring her that we would be her support. In the meantime as I try countless times to contact her son, I continuously get his voicemail. I left message after message until finally I told his mother that he would not return my calls. She went on to say that her son was in denial and the enemy of his soul knew that. But I knew that God was ready to snatch him from the fire. A few weeks passed by and I still had not gotten in touch with him but I was determined to inspire this young man. One day in the late spring of 2006, I received a call from the young man. I was caught off guard when my caller ID displayed his name and number. I didn't actually expect him to ever call. I introduced myself and explained that his mother and I attend the same church. All of a sudden the phone went dead. The brother actually hung up on me. But I knew it was nothing but the enemy of his soul and I still needed to press on. Several hours later he called me back. This time we had a conversation. He said, "listen man, I need a job. I don't know why she told you to call me. I'm alright". I explained to the brother that all I wanted to do was to help him. He asked if I could get him a job. I told him that it was possible. So we continued to talk and gain one another's trust. The Lord had actually lead me to the same person I was just four years ago. Broken, sick and without faith. His mother told me that he was over

6 feet tall but only weighed about 120 pounds soaking wet. He was literally skin and bones. But this is the same young man who told me that he was alright. I thought to myself, boy doesn't that sound familiar. Those were the exact words that I spoke before I gained faith. I finally convinced him to come to church with me. I can still remember that Friday evening when we met for the first time, face to face. He indeed resembled me pre transplant in that he was skin and bones, drawn and weak. He was ready to receive God. He asked me to go and get one of the pastors to pray over him. We really enjoyed that evening of worship. We even stayed outside in the rain to converse for 40 minutes after service was over. After that the young man would call daily to check on me. His spirit had done a complete 360 and things were starting to take shape in his life. He had gotten himself an apartment and the Lord had blessed him with a job. I spoke with him in the month of July and told him that my family and I were going on vacation but we would speak when I got back. At that time I inquired about his ability to receive one of his mother's kidneys. He informed me that even though he was now prepared spiritually he was not medically cleared. He told me that he was taking medication for a hereditary heart condition but that he would be off the medicine by January. He was sick and tired of

dialysis and couldn't wait until January to finally get the transplant. I never got the chance to speak with him again. When I returned from vacation I became consumed with other things and before I realized it, the summer was just about over. As my family and I were preparing to celebrate my wife's birthday and my four-year transplant anniversary on September 1st, the telephone rang. It was my young friend's mother. She informed me that her son had taken a turn for the worse. She went on to say that he flat lined twice and was hanging on for dear life. My mood quickly became somber. The devil always wants to steal your joy. I made several visits to the hospital to see him but he was always heavily sedated. I prayed over him and I prayed with his mother in hopes that he would pull through. Two weeks went by and his health began to improve. But on September 26th, of 2006 at or about 5 am, Delfonte went home to be with the Lord. When his mother called me and told me the news, my initial reaction was of sadness. I quickly wiped away my tears because I knew in my heart and soul that God had prepared a place for my young friend. After the funeral was over there was a weight on my shoulders. As I drove home, I wondered if I had failed this young man. Then I went on to ask myself would it have been better for me to have never known him or to have met him and he passed away from this Earth only 90 days after meeting him. It worried my soul. Those burdens only lasted briefly because I remembered that night when we rejoiced at the Cathedral in Perth Amboy, New Jersey. He had truly found the Lord, so I knew he was prepared to be received. I continue to walk and inspire those who are in need. I just thank God for the path that he has chosen for me to walk.

After reading and understanding what God has done in my life. All things are possible to those who believeth. God will never give you more than you can bear. I want to thank God for giving me one more chance. Our level of faith will either make us triumphant or make our lives a tragedy.

Chapter 9

A Changed Life

One day as I was putting my daughter on the school bus the Holy Spirit convicted me. I was directed to end my book with the testimonies of the lives of those who had been changed by the events of what you just read. God had spoken to me and told me that he will direct me to the individuals who will write this chapter of this book.

Deacon Albert J. Daily III
Cathedral International

I am still awe struck that I was chosen to be a part of this great work. Prior to being asked by Brother Calloway to write a section in this book, I only knew him to be a noticeably favored man of God who had joined the Fruit of Jesus Security Ministry under my leadership. I found him to be faithful in his commitment to serve. He was also full of testimony in his mouth as he greeted and served with his Brothers and Sisters in the Ministry on a regular basis.

I can recall several years ago, seeing the pictures that were taken of him during his illness on the big screen one evening during a Thursday night Bible Study at Cathedral International. After sharing his pictures with everyone in attendance that evening, he then walked down the center aisle showing everyone that the Lord had indeed done it again. God had brought forth life from death and healing from sickness! I was amazed to see in person what the Chief Physician Jesus Christ had done with and to this brother. He had the appearance of a man who had never been sick yet alone one who was on his death bed, not too long before that evening.

Brother Calloway called me one evening to tell me that the Lord had told him to ask me to write a section in his upcoming book. What could I say but yes! Not only was I excited but also I was grateful and honored to be considered. He began to read a few chapters to me over the phone and I must say that I felt the presence of the Lord in all that he read. As he read the words from hand written and typed pages of notes of his awesome life story, the Lord began to show me visions of what was to come not only to him but to those that read his book and listen to his story. Everything that I shared with Brother Calloway about what the Lord was showing me was confirmation to what the Lord had already spoken and shown him. We were amazed that God had chosen us both. We then began to say to one another, "why not me"?

As I type this section, Bother Calloway has been a walking and living testimony of the healing power of the Lord Jesus Christ he is also concerned about giving back to others. He is a mentor for troubled youths, does public speaking on a regular basis, promotes organ donation, referees track and field events and foremost is a wonderful husband and father. The world will be blessed when God brings Brother Calloway's testimony and story before the masses. He is destined to tell the good news of the Lord's healing power and mercy. He also wants to share the fact that he was given another chance to make things right with the Lord. All I can say is nothing but God. Press on my Brother, press on!

Elna "Bunny" Chanley (neighbor)

I had just come home from visiting Anwar (Anthony) in the hospital and headed straight for his house where I knew his mother in law was watching his kids. I was angry and upset and told her that if his illness didn't kill him I would.

Anwar (Anthony) had spent the entire time I was with him complaining about everything and everybody – his nurses left him there alone for too long, they never came when he buzzed for them, the food was terrible or cold, his pillows were not right – the television didn't work right. Karen didn't spend enough time with him; she was always running to do something with the kids. He made me wonder why anyone would want to visit him at all. The nurses began to keep him sedated to keep him quiet – and as sick as he was he knew that was what they were doing. I remember when I first met Anwar (Anthony) the thing that impressed me most about him was his quick wit, wonderful easy laugh and his ability to make others laugh and feel good. He was always ready and available to his family, friends and neighbors with whatever they needed, with a good sense of humor and never a complaint.

Anwar (Anthony) is a Marine and before his illness looked like a billboard ad for men's well-fitted jeans or underwear. When he began to lose a lot of weight and his smile did not come so quickly we knew something was really wrong.

After many doctor visits and tests it was determined his liver was not functioning properly. Family and friends took turns taking him back and forth to his doctors, Riverview Hospital or the Philadelphia Hospital or wherever it was that he needed to go.

None of us could understand this onset of illness; which took hold of Anwar (Anthony) with a vengeance. He never drank alcohol other than socially, never smoked, never did drugs- he respected and took care of his body and health – so why was this happening to him. He became so weak he was unable to take care of himself. He had to be fed, bathed, dressed and cared for twenty-four seven. He was not even able to turn himself over in bed; he could not even take himself to the bathroom. He couldn't' sit at the kitchen table. He could hardly ride in the car. He had to ride lying down. He really dreaded riding in the car with me. I drove too slow for him and by the time we got to where we were going his temper was stretched to the max. He lost weight so quickly he became just skin and bones. The hospital nurses couldn't find a vein that they could use to give him a blood transfusion. All his power of self-reliance had been taken from him and he was at the mercy of everyone else. He slept so much of the time we all felt he would die any minute.

There were the long trips to the Philadelphia Hospital to visit him. He just wanted to come home and be with his family – they were never pleasant or even hopeful visits. But we went because we needed to show him how much he meant to us and to keep up his moral up as much as possible. There was nothing any of us could do but standby and watch him deteriorate and pray the professionals were able to do something to help ease his pain. Luckily, I was there one day when a new doctor came to visit. He was questioning how his diagnosis had been determined and wrote in his chart that it was due to alcoholism and race, thinking this had been erroneously omitted on his chart. He didn't fit their profile for this diagnosis (cryptogenic cirrhosis). I told him if you put (alcohol cirrhosis) in his chart it will be a permanent part of his record and it was not correct. So he must fix the record. I trust he did that, but it just goes to show that some people have a prejudged notion that if you have liver disease you must be an alcoholic, especially if; you are a black male.

Eventually Anwar (Anthony) was released and sent home to die.

Anwar (Anthony) had other ideas- if he was going to die he wanted to give Karen something for their anniversary that she could remember. As weak as he was, he planned a cruise. They were to leave for Mexico and on July 8, 2002 he got a phone call that there was a compatible liver available and he needed to be at TJU within three hours. Anwar determined that it was not the right time for him and told the doctors and nurses so, they tried to convince him that he should accept the liver, he said, "not this time". He went on his cruise to celebrate his love for Karen and their anniversary. It turned out to be the trip from "HELL". When they returned Anwar's (Anthony's) health had deteriorated even further, if that was possible. It became a matter of waiting, either for him to die or for a new liver to become available.

We held group prayer for him at his house often. Sometimes there were 20 or 30 family members and friends holding hands and offering Anwar (Anthony) up to God's will. We praised God for his presence in our midst and we also prayed for comfort and a miracle. We asked God to hold Karen and their children, Niya, Jihad and Nigeria, to comfort them and strengthen them in their time of need. We put our faith in God's hand.

Soon there afterwards, I got a call saying they were going to the hospital. They had gotten a call and I was told that Anwar (Anthony) was ready for whatever God had in store for him. They say Karen had fainted when she got the call but she too placed her future in God's hand. So off they went. It was a long ride from what I was told, tension and fear ran high and Marvin drove them most of the way in silence. Anwar's (Anthony's) mother–in-law and the rest of us stayed behind waiting. Anwar (Anthony) was so thin and weak that no one was sure that he would make it to see another day, but the doctor's felt that they had to try. The doctor's knew that the time was critical and they got the job done in record time. The next phone call was to say that Anwar (Anthony) came through the operation. He was alive and stable. Praise God!

The long journey to recovery was no easier to go through than before the operation and Anwar (Anthony) wanted everything in a hurry. He rushed his healing and didn't waist any time getting back on his feet as soon as he was able.

But Anwar (Anthony) was not the same person, he had changed, his whole attitude and demeanor was different. He was quieter and more serious and driven. He felt he had to give back to God, all he had been given, which was his life, his health, his family, his power.

So today we see a different, but the same, loving, caring beautiful person. He has put off the old and taken on the new and God is at the beginning and the end in his life.

Anwar (Anthony) has made such a difference in my life. Teaching me patience, understanding and increasing my faith in God, life and people. I have turned friends and acquaintances into family and feel loved and blessed to be a part of their lives.

The life and death of Caroline, the young woman whose liver lives within Anwar (Anthony) will never be forgotten. She lives on as she and Anwar (Anthony) continue their journey of life together and they will meet each other on the other side when their journey together is finished.

Anwar (Anthony) continues to be serious but the laughter and the helpfulness has returned. Through it is tough to continue the many medications and the doctor visits still continue, Anwar (Anthony) knows these are the earthly things that help to keep him going in this physical world. Beside we all made it quite clear to him that we cannot go through this experience again anytime soon, if ever. The love that surrounds him and even the anger when he feels he does not need to take his medication is the spiritual unseen. These things are a sign of God's love and caring for us. We need to remember that God can dream a greater dream for us than we can dream for ourselves. All we have to do is believe and reach out for it and have faith in God's plan for us.

Anwar (Anthony) you are my brother and I love you. You and your family have given me more than you will ever know and I too am a part of all you are. Live long, live healthy, and live wisely. You have a vision for yourself, but God has a greater vision for you and if you let him, he will lead you to places you only dare dream to go.

Kristine Alfund (director youth advocate program)

I have known Anthony for about a year and a half and have only known him as a warm-hearted, caring man. Anthony has told me about his life before his liver transplant and it was hard for me to believe that he was much different. As he was telling me about it, I was in awe and trying to picture him as someone who was capable of not caring about others. Needless to say, I was unable to visualize something so foreign to the Anthony that I know.

Anthony told me the "Second Chance at Life" story that he endured and as he was telling it I felt myself tear up. He is truly a survivor and has made great strides. After hearing how God had changed his priorities in life and he started volunteering for the N.J. Sharing Network and started speaking about organ donation, I signed up as a donor. Knowing that one day there may be a possibility that I could help someone the way Anthony was helped has really inspired me.

Anthony is an exceptional Behavioral Assistant/Mentor and has touched many children's lives with his wisdom and caring heart. All the families that he has worked with have seen positive changes in their children and view him as a tremendous role model. I am honored that he is giving back to the community and helping the families in our program.

Thank you for all of your hard work and dedication; the families you work with and the YAP staff in Monmouth County appreciate it. Anthony my hopes are that at least one person will read your book and it will change their life.

Curtis "Muke" Aquil (best friend)

In my life, I have heard of Miracles; read of Miracles and even prayed for Miracles. It was not until the events leading up to and culminating in the successful liver transplant of a dear friend of mine, that I had witnessed" first hand" could only be a miracle from God………..since that I now not only pray for miracles…I have come to expect them.

I would like to take the opportunity to share with the reader a truly extraordinary story…. A story involving the witnessing of a miracle that took place Aug of 2002. A miracle that saved the life of my dear friend and brother…. Anthony"Anwar"Calloway of Newark, New Jersey.

It was clear and sunny day in Aug 2002. We had planned a: "short fuse" trip to New Jersey to see Anwar (Anthony) for what could have realistically been the last time. I base this on my conversation with his wife Karen as well as my last conversation with Anwar (Anthony), which was not much of a conversation due to his severe decline in health.

It was after my last conversation with both Anwar (Anthony) and Karen, and during the days leading up to our trip to New Jersey that I began to ponder the possibility that Anwar (Anthony) may not win this long and debilitating battle that he had so gallantly fought over the course of two years. I even began to think about such things as what I would possibly say at his funeral. You see the fact of the matter was that I was experiencing a form of denial…that there was no way that Anwar (Anthony) could possibly be dying from this terrible liver disease. I think it was easier for me to be in denial since I was living in the state of Virginia and did not see Anwar (Anthony) on a frequent basis as others did, and certainly not on a daily basis as his wife Karen did. To this day I am still in awe at the strength and perseverance she displayed throughout the whole ordeal. She is truly a remarkable woman.

During the drive up from Virginia we received a call on the cell phone from Karen stating that she had just received a call from Thomas

Jefferson Hospital regarding a liver match for Anwar (Anthony). They were rushing frantically to get on the road and she asked if we could redirect and meet them at the hospital. Both my wife and I were in shock at the news as I turned around and headed for Thomas Jefferson Hospital in Philadelphia P.A.

While driving to the hospital I was nearly overwhelmed by the thought that this had to be "Divine" Intervention at work and that everything would be fine.

We arrived at Thomas Jefferson Hospital that afternoon shortly before Anwar (Anthony) arrived under escort by his wife and her father.

Opening the door of the vehicle and seeing my friend sitting there helpless I could not help from feeling sad. What I saw was a merely a shell of the individual who was once full of life and verve. The feeling of sadness was quickly set aside and replaced with the excitement and anticipation that the stage was being set for Anwar (Anthony) to finally have his liver transplant and thus have his life saved.

Prior to this day, on more than one occasion, I told Karen that when the time came for Anwar (Anthony) to have his transplant that I wanted to be there…I never felt she really understood how strongly I felt about this. It is the feeling you have of waiting to be there for a friend in his time of need.

With the help of his father in-law, we lifted Anwar (Anthony) from the vehicle and on to a wheel chair where I proceeded to wheel him into the emergency room. It was a high honor and privilege to be there for my friend when he was most in need. I feel that it was no coincidence that fate would have it this way. After all, Anwar (Anthony) and I go way back indeed.

I would be remiss if I didn't mention that while in the process of getting Anwar (Anthony) admitted to the Emergency room, I had an opportunity to speak to another old friend (Wayne "Wali" Lewis) who called to offer well wishes and prayers…he also told me that since I was there with Anwar (Anthony), his mind was at ease and he knew that everything was going to turn out fine. It felt good to hear and was most reassuring at a time when everyone was looking for any and all signs of reassurance.

The mood in the emergency room was typical. There were many lab technicians and medical personnel moving about in the usual way medical personnel do. Anwar (Anthony) had the normal in-processing procedures of drawing blood, taking vitals etc…it was not until a nurse working directly with the transplant team arrived that the mood in the emergency room actually took on the appearance of an emergency in process.

As I studied the look on the face of this particular nurse it finally dawned on me that this transplant was going to take place regardless of the results of Anwar's (Anthony's) current blood work. In fact, it was apparent that the blood work as well as the other Emergency Room in-processing procedures; were merely a formality. It further became clear when the anesthesiologist explained that basically time was of the essence and that the transplant liver was reaching a point where if not transplanted soon then the liver would more than likely fail.

As I listened to the anesthesiologist explain the situation, it further validated what I felt in my heart upon seeing Anwar (Anthony) as he arrived at the hospital…and that was his moment…his date with destiny if you will. It became clear that this was it…one shot, one opportunity…do or die.

From that moment on, for me the situation became surreal. At times like this so many thoughts flash through your mind. For me, I could not help but to think how it was possible that something like this could happen to Anwar (Anthony). I also felt that if anyone could pull through and make it then it would be Anwar (Anthony).

As the mood in the Emergency room became more intense; Medical personnel began to work in a more urgent manner. Within minutes Anwar (Anthony) was removed from the Emergency room area. He was whisked away on a gurney in route to the operating room.

The group of us; Karen, Karen's father, and myself escorted Anwar (Anthony) with Medical personnel as far as we could go (which was the operating room Waiting area). It was during this passage that Anwar (Anthony) for the first time since his arrival at the hospital that day, voluntarily spoke. The words that came out of his mouth were foreign to everyone in attendance with the exception of me. The words he spoke were actually the words from an old Marine Corps War Song:

> You can have your Army Khakis'
>
> You can have your Navy Blues
>
> But here's a different "fighting man"
>
> I'll introduce to you…His uniform is different
>
> from any you've ever seen
>
> The Germans called him Devil Dog
>
> His title is Marine…………
>
> Marine…
>
> Marine…
>
> His real name is "Marine"

It was at that moment that I knew that Anwar (Anthony) was ready to do what he had to do, and that was to fight. It was at that moment in time that I felt deep in my heart that this new found spirit he had was part of the miracle that was taking place before us all.

As we reached the point where we had to say farewell to Anwar (Anthony), before they took him into the operating room…I shall never forget the look in his eyes. It was not a look of fear, nor was it a look of sadness or defeat. The look was one that could only come from the type of suffering that he had experienced over the long course of this ordeal. The look in his eyes was the look of one who was ready and determine to beat the odds and do what ever it took to survive.

As we all waited patiently in the waiting area, the mood amongst us all was very somber but positive. Our mood was further reinforced by the periodic "good news" we were receiving from the medical support personnel assisting in the transplant.

The first bit of good news we received was that the "Old" liver was removed without complication. The medical personnel informed us that the "Old liver was in very bad shape and definitely needed to be removed.

The second bit of good news we received was that the actual transplant was going very well and at the rate they were going surgery would probably be done shortly, which from what we were told was a very good sign.

The next bit of "great" news that we received came at approximately 12:00am, when we were told that the transplant was a success and that the lead surgeon would be out to speak with us shortly.

At approximately 1:30am the Doctor was seen approaching us from the long passageway. She briefed us on the surgery and told us that it went extremely well. She answered a few questions and concluded by informing us that we would be able to see Anwar (Anthony) in Post Op shortly.

At approximately 3:45am, I took my turn to visit Anwar (Anthony) in the Post Op room he was assigned to. It had only been a couple of hours since he had his new liver, but it appeared, at least to me that he was already starting to look better.

As I gazed out at the bright lights overlooking the city of Philadelphia; I couldn't help but to reminisce of days long gone…days when me and my friend use to party with the best of them……….it was Wine, Women, and Song back in those days.

Looking at those bright lights, I thought to myself…one of these days when Anwar (Anthony) is fully recovered, that we would definitely have to return to the city of "Brotherly Love" under much different circumstances.

As I look at Anwar (Anthony) lying there hooked up to the breathing apparatus, I could not help but think how close he came to death while thanking God Almighty that he was given another chance at life.

It's been a few years since that fateful day in Aug of 2002. I am both humbled and inspired by the event surrounding Anwar's (Anthony's) transplant and his new lease on life. I truly believe that certain things happen for reasons not obvious to man. Anthony "Anwar" Calloway not only has a changed life……………………..he has a better life.

Solomon, Patricia, Solomon Jr., Simone
The Simpkins Family (neighbors)

We first met Anthony two years ago when we exchanged hellos while putting our kids on the school bus. We didn't know it then but he had been sent into our lives for a reason. After listening to Anthony's testimony and seeing his pictures I truly felt that he was a miracle standing before us. God had granted Anthony a second chance at life. Here today and gone tomorrow was something that we always believed but now we can say that we have bared witness to the miracle.

Anthony's wife Karen is a blessing, a true gift from God. In Anthony's time of need, her relationship with God helped bring Anthony closer to God. She was there to help him receive his blessing.

Anthony you and your family came into our family's life at a time when it was most needed. One might call it "The Cross Roads". Yours is a family of angels and our family was searching for the righteousness that your experience helped us find.

At the time when we met, our family was attending church but not getting much out of it. When we expressed this to you, you extended an invitation for us to visit your church, Cathedral International in Perth Amboy. It was electrifying to hear Anthony speak about church. There was so much passion behind every word he said. His excitement was something you couldn't falsify; this was genuine praise to God. His passion and enthusiasm is contagious. We visited the Cathedral and soon after became members. Cathedral International has changed our lives and it has changed for the best.

Anthony and Karen you are truly a blessing as well as a miracle, keep spreading God's word and may God bless and keep you.

Georgina, John, Anne-Marie, Dawn, Tim, Lauren, Bobby, and Travis (Donor Family)

August 28, 2002

Just like every other day, my sister Caroline went to the Medallion Center- the place she enjoyed more than anything. Caroline wasn't feeling well. I wanted her to stay home, but she insisted on going. She was determined not to miss the special lunch planned at the center. I gave in to her not knowing it would be the last time I would see or talk to her.

I had called the director on staff at the Center that morning about Caroline not feeling well. He wouldn't be available until 12:00 noon to talk with me. When the telephone rang right after lunch, I had expected it to be the doctor. This call changed my life completely and is one that I will never forget.

Caroline's counselor, told me Caroline had passed out and they had started CPR. My initial reaction was to question why CPR was being done if she had passed out. After telling the counselor I was on my way, I ran through the house to awaken my husband. On the way to the Center, I called the counselor back on my cell phone. My heart was racing, but I was sure everything would be alright.

It seemed like forever before we arrived at the Center. The ambulance had arrived. The Director of the Center met my husband and me. He proceeded to tell me that Caroline had a choking accident and was unconscious for a very long time. At that point, we followed the ambulance to the hospital.

At the emergency entrance, I was finally able to see Caroline. I knew she was in bad condition. It was a few minutes later when the grief nurse came to talk with us. Caroline was in grave condition. They never said she had passed away that would be days away. I remember being in Caroline's room trying everything to wake her up. But, she was gone. God had already taken her from us. The machines were now keeping her alive.

The Sharing Network visited us to discuss organ donation. After several family meetings, we made the decision to donate Caroline's organs. Since Caroline never smoked, she was strong, and in good health we hoped her organs might help someone else. My family and I stayed with Caroline every day and prayed for her. We remembered how she loved life and her obsessions with shopping, coloring, and crafts. She liked spending time with her family and friends. She had the most contagious laugh. These last few days were the hardest days of our lives. Caroline died on August 30, 2002.

The year after Caroline's death was extremely difficult time for our family. Holidays were especially hard since Caroline enjoyed and planned them months in advance. As the one-year anniversary neared, the Sharing Network sent an invitation for a memorial and requested each family create a quilt in remembrance of their loved one. Even after a year, I didn't feel I was ready. With the help and encouragement of my family, I decided to attend. My granddaughter came up with the design and the two of us made the 12x12 quilt square in memory of Caroline. I had no idea how our lives were going to change as we prepared before the memorial, I received an anonymous letter. It was from the wife of the person who received Caroline's liver. She had written to tell us about her husband and family, and how her husband became ill. She expressed her thanks to our family for saving her husband's life and her hopes in meeting our family. My family was both moved and happy to receive her letter. We decided to wait until after the memorial to contact the Sharing Network and work through them to meet Caroline's organ recipient. But God had his own plans.

The day of the memorial came and I was hesitant about going. I was not sure I was ready to remember Caroline so soon after her death. With my family by my side, I went to the memorial. As we waited for the memorial service to begin, my daughters noticed the organ recipient guest speakers listed in the program. One of them was a liver recipient. My daughters asked me what I would do if the speaker happened to be the recipient of Caroline's liver. I didn't believe there was a chance this person received Caroline's organ. During the service we heard from family members who had lost loved ones, both young and old, that had donated their organs. I was very moved by their stories. Being at the memorial brought back so many memories of Caroline. We then heard from the organ recipients, including Anthony Calloway. When Anthony began to tell his story, we realized that he was in fact the person who had received Caroline's liver. All of the details he shared with the group were the same as what we had just read in the anonymous letter received just days before. My husband asked me what was I going to do. I started shaking and crying and didn't know what to do. At this point in the service, we were all asked to light candles in memory of the person we had lost. I decided that I would go over to Anthony and light his candle. I walked over to the Calloway family, blew out Anthony's candle and relit it as I put my hands on his cheek and said, "This is from my sister, Caroline." I went back to my seat and cried. I wanted the service to be over so that I could tell them about my family and Caroline.

Through the remainder of the service, Anthony's wife kept looking at my family. She had thought that I was a person overcome by grief or someone just completely crazy! Once over, my family and I made our way over to Anthony and his family. I walked over to Anthony's wife, Karen and told her that I received her letter. In my hand was the anonymous letter. She looked at the letter and realized it was the one she had sent to the donor family. Karen and I hugged and cried. She kept thanking me for saving her husband's life. Anthony came over at this point he had no idea what had taken place. Karen told Anthony that we were his donor family and that we received their letter. Everyone in each family hugged and cried. We shared Caroline's quilt with the Calloway's and spent some time sharing memories of Caroline with them. No one at the service could believe that a miracle happened; not even the Sharing Network staff who arranged the event. On this day, we met a very special family a devoted father, husband, and now my brother. We met my sister's liver recipient.

I lost a sister whom I loved very much and continue to miss every day. But through her death, I have been given a loving, caring brother and a whole new, extended family. Since our chance meeting at the memorial, our families continue to grow and spent time together. We have created new memories together. Caroline would have loved Anthony, Karen, Jihad and Niya. She always wanted children and now she is a part of a wonderful family.

My family and I are proud of Anthony and all he is doing with his new life. As a mentor to youths and his work with the transplant team, he is helping to get information out on donor awareness. Anthony, our brother, we are proud and love you with all of our hearts. We wish you continued good health, happiness, and success with your inspirational voice. Thank you for being a part of our lives.

Love,
Your sister, Georgina, John, Anne-Marie,
Dawn, Tim, Lauren, Bobby, and Travis
(Donor Family)

Niya (daughter)

My dad was getting sick and I didn't understand why mommy was crying so much. Dad was in the hospital all the time and he didn't look the same anymore. My mom told me to pray and I did…. real hard. I can remember Grandma Helen coming to me in a dream and telling me daddy would be alright. I remember mommy letting me lead prayer when all the family came over. They said that I sure knew how to pray. God heard my prayers and I never forget to thank God daily for his never ending love and mercy. My dad is different now and he takes the time to run and play with me. He is also involved in my school and helps me in my school all the time. My dad is also the best soccer coach ever. I love my dad and God has changed our lives because he healed my dad.

Jihad (son)

I just remember my dad being sick one day. He was so cruel to me. He would command me to do this and do that. I asked God why my family was being destroyed like this? My mom would tell me to never question God and we must pray for God's healing power. My sister and I layed in the bed with my mom at night and we prayed for my dad to get better. I wanted everything to be alright again. I know that God can change things because my dad is healthy now. He is a great dad and I love him. He plays basketball with my friends and me and he always challenges me in a video game or two. God does answer prayers. I have seen the miracle that he has done.

Nigeria (daughter)

Due to the circumstances my father was in, I am very pleased that God has blessed him to see another day, and watch his children, and his grandchild grow up. Life is very short and I am so glad that my Father got a second chance to appreciate every moment of what was taken for granted. Live long my father; Dante and I love you dearly.

Karen (wife)

The monitors were blaring. The doctors were pumping blood in his body and his blood pressure was continuing to drop. I began prayer once again as I had done countless times before. I didn't know what God's plan was for my husband and I certainly couldn't imagine life without him. I now realize today that God not only had a plan for his life but through this experience my life certainly would be different. I have learned that God needed something new to take place in my life. I told Anthony constantly that he needed to have the faith of a "mustard seed". I would speak this to him daily but at times I didn't believe myself. You see my faith was being tested and I didn't even know it. I had to "appear" that I had it all together. There were times when I felt so weak and vulnerable. To tell you the truth I was afraid and the devil was trying to step in. I pressed on, continued to pray and knew that I needed to be strong for my husband and my kids. I had to hold on to that "mustard seed" faith because believe me that was all that I had. Hebrews 11:1 states that faith is the substance of things hoped for and the evidence of things unseen. I would sing this song daily but I needed to see something fast because I was growing weary and tired. I held on and even though times were getting rough I learned that the devil was a liar and I could not give him the victory by giving up on my husband. I am now a changed woman in Christ. I have learned what it is to "expect" God and know that God can change things. That storm in my life is over and I have learned to praise him through the good and the bad. I am truly grateful that my husband and I are now one with Christ. We can do all things through Christ who strengthens us.

This concludes the Chapter of a Changed Life. I hope that you have been inspired by what you have just read. God has truly placed favor on my life, and if I had a thousand tongues I could not praise God enough.

Psalm 136:1 Give thanks to the Lord, for he is good

Matthew 7:7,8 Ask and it will be given to you; seek and you will find, knock and the door will be opened to you. For everyone who asks receives; he who seeks find; and to him who knocks; the door will be opened.

Be Blessed

The End.

Thank you

I can't thank you all enough for being so good to me, without your help oh God where would I be.

You sacrificed a part of yourself sometimes until late at night, you gave me so much encouragement when the end seemed nowhere in sight.

God surrounded you all around me for reasons I just don't know, you helped me to be a better person surely I have grown.

Thank you, thank you, and thank you, for being by my side, your good deeds will not be forgotten my arms are open wide.

To all who helped in any way!

Printed in the United States
78823LV00005BA/319-348